The Special Needs Ministry Handbook

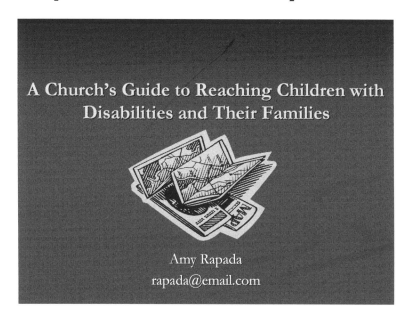

A Church's Guide to Reaching Children with Disabilities and Their Families

Amy Rapada
rapada@email.com

© 2007
CGR Publishing
Third Printing, 2007

Love and great thanks to my wonderful husband, Cal and amazing daughter Emily for their support always~

Scripture quoted from
The Holy Bible, New International Version
by International Bible Society
© 2007

United States Copyright Certificate of Registration Number: TXu 1-058-827
The Library of Congress Copyright Office

Dedicated to Zach, who is my inspiration
for this ministry

And to all families with specials needs for
their ongoing commitment to their children
may they have complete faith in God
throughout the journey...

Amy Rapada
© 2007 by Amy Rapada

Table of Contents

 *Prologue*

A Journey of Faith- "The Power went out, but God's Light Stayed On"

(*A true story of my child's neurodegenerative disease and God's powerful ability to generate special needs ministries throughout churches*)

I continue to be impressed by the genuine interest that many have taken in special needs ministries. I am humbled to be writing on the topic of children with disabilities and awed by God's ever presence in my life. God has blessed me, and He will bless you in this ministry as well.

If you allow Him to, I believe that God can have a powerful impact on your life through that special child or family that has led you to pick up this book. Perhaps He is asking you to open your eyes, your heart and your mind, to the special needs population. Ninety five percent of those with disabilities are currently "unchurched". With this in mind, let us all embrace differences throughout our religious communities and in doing so bring others to see His light.

Almost 20 years ago, my husband and I planned our wedding to be held in Seattle, Washington. Printed on the cover of our ceremony program was the Bible verse, Romans 8:28: **"For I know the plans that I have for you...that all things will work together for good, for those that love the Lord their God."** If we love God, He will bring good out of every situation.

A first grade teacher at the time of our marriage, I invited my whole class of students to sing in the wedding. As we entered the beautiful sanctuary, one of my students with disabilities tapped me on the shoulder. It was the first time he had ever been in a church. With wide eyes, he gazed around and in wonderment said, "I like God's House." *The church* is God's House. *Your church*, or the building where you congregate to worship God, is God's House. Picture Him welcoming in His children. He would welcome in any child, no matter how severe the physical, mental, emotional or behavioral dysfunction. God loves His children as they are. **"Whoever welcomes one of these children in My name welcomes Me," reads Mark 9:37. Written directly in the Bible, this is the special needs mission.**

Most churches want very much to welcome children with disabilities, but often aren't sure how to accommodate their needs. Setting up a special needs ministry allows us to reach out to and care for these families in their times of trials. It allows special families to let God guide and carry them through their daily struggles. **"God is close to the broken hearted and those that are crushed in spirit" says Psalm 34:18. Verse 19 continues: "A righteous man may have many troubles, but God will see him through them all."**

God began to make this mission clear to me when my son, Zach was 4 ½ years and my daughter Emily just 6 months. God had blessed us with two healthy and typically developing children. Everyday was filled with teaching them a new skill and seeing them quickly learn it. At that time, Zach was trying to master (to perfection) the ability to "pump" his legs while swinging on our outdoor swing set. It was while practicing this "in and out" rhythmic motion that he looked up at me and asked, "Mom, will you always help me?" "Yes", I replied happily, not realizing the impact that my words would come to hold.

Just days later, began the onset of a rare disease, inexplicable seizures, loss of skills and many questions about how to help our son. Ten years thus far, a promise is being fulfilled, while God's plan to help others through Zach continues to unfold.

In the beginning, it was hard to see what God's plan was. The first years were extremely difficult. We watched our healthy, smiling and verbal child slip further from us each day. His speech, motor skills, and facial expressions were diminishing. We witnessed personality changes, physical stroke like episodes and dementia type behaviors. We missed him. We longed to see him play creatively and laugh again. Most of all, we missed having conversations with him.

We saw physician after physician, specialist after specialist, expert after expert, and repeated test after test. There were no answers. "Our son was a puzzle," we were told. He must have a rare condition, perhaps one that had not yet been discovered. We poured over books, scoured the internet, made all kinds of phone calls and even traveled to other states for advice. Still no answers…

At one desperate moment, I found myself at the local pediatrician's office. With no appointment, I sped past the receptionist desk, two children in hand, to tell our family doctor that there had been a mistake. "This was not supposed to happen to our child and something needed to be done to fix him immediately." Quietly, she guided me to a back room, sat me down calmly and explained that while we didn't know the cause, "something life altering had occurred." She was right. Our lives have never been the same since. In fact, it was at that moment that a journey of learning and deeper faith began.

God does not make mistakes and He always has answers. His groundwork was being laid and His plans would very gradually be shown to us. We now became even more immersed in the world of health care: physical, occupational, speech, sign language, sensory, music, play, water and even horseback riding therapy became a part of the rehabilitation process. Neurologists, Epileptologists, Psychologists, Neuro-Psychiatrists, Kidney Specialists, EEG, MRI and CAT scan Technicians, Nutritionists, and Special Educators consumed our lives.

At several points, there were some partial remissions for our son. Speech was recovered for just a short period of time, long enough for him to tell us, as he clutched his head tightly **"*the power went out.*"** *"The power went out"* he *proclaimed with a perplexed look on his face. This was his way of telling us that his thinking, his socializing, and his movement* channels *had been cut off.* **God's power, though, could not go out.**

In order to keep God's power shining brightly in our lives, we needed more than ever, to stay "plugged in" to our church. For a couple of years, every Sunday my husband and I team taught our son's Sunday school class. I did the teaching, while my husband assisted our son. The children in the class were respectful of our child's differences and of course had questions. One child asked why Zach no longer spoke her language. Another wanted to know why he colored the way he did. His art work had taken a scribble format. We did our best to explain that while Zach's abilities had changed, God loved him the same as He always had. After the lesson, we noticed that a curious number of students had created pictures to include a bit of scribbling.

The following year, our son's condition had worsened. Volunteers came to our home so that we could attend worship service. While it was much appreciated, our goal was to allow our son to return to Sunday school. In the summer of 2000, I literally felt a light go on in my mind. God, the great generator had sent a bright source of power. I drove immediately to my church to share this spark of information.

Met by Sue Craik, our newly chosen director of Children's Ministries, I shared with her the idea to begin a special needs program. (I had recently served on the hiring committee that selected Sue as Children's Minister). One of the things that I liked then and now about Sue is that she herself is a vibrant energizer. I had no sooner expressed the thought and she said, "Let's do it." Now, she could have very easily said, "we only have one special needs child here," or "it's not in our budget," or "we don't have the space," or simply "we're not ready for that." **God is ready for us to do!** When we do nothing, nothing happens. When we do something and the purpose of that something is to glorify God, amazing things happen**.**

I began that summer calling on volunteers, one by one, and telling them about my son's condition. I was overjoyed to find that there were many skillful and compassionate people who came forward when they knew that there was a need. Whether you are beginning with just one special needs child or a number of children, I encourage you to seek out and personally invite others to join you in this ministry. Educators, health care professionals, therapists, support persons, typical peers...they are in your churches**. This is a church wide mission**. When we, as a church, adopt the idea that we will put a special needs ministry into place, we will be amazed at the families that God will send to us. We will be touched by these blessed children and inspired by their courageous parents.

I'm honored to tell you about some families that I have come to know as a result of the special needs ministry.

Jordan was three when his Dad carried him down the church aisle excitedly to tell me that this was their first visit to a church that had a special needs ministry. "I think we're in the right place," he said. Jordan has cerebral palsy, as well as a beaming smile and sharp mind.

Abby was five when she and her Mom began driving a good hour and a half each way to participate in the special needs class. Arriving first in her wheelchair and in later days her walker, Abby's happy nature tells everyone that she is eager to learn about and sing praises to God.

Alexander and Raphael are brothers, ages 12 and 13. Both have autism. Their Mom, a family medicine physician, has many resources to help them, yet she was not able to find a Sunday school for them. It had been 10 years since she had worshipped at church.

Nicolas was 6 at the start of this ministry. He continues to participate wholeheartedly in both the regular and special needs "reverse inclusion" program. Having mild deficits, Nick is a model to many of the special needs students. His parents say that he feels safe in the special needs classroom.

Evan, now age 11, is highly gifted. His Asperger's syndrome made it difficult for him to cope socially in the regular Sunday school class. The specifically tailored special needs class, with many typical peers, encouraged Evan's unique abilities. Eventually, Evan was able to be successful in the regular Sunday school program. He shared with us one Sunday that he would one day "be a great orator of God," or he would "be in the food industry."

Andrew was four when he was diagnosed with both Asperger's syndrome and attention deficit disorder. His Mom bravely changed churches, so that he could do well in a church school environment. An endearing child, I picture him jumping on the mini trampoline and eating snacks (but not at the same time☺).

Hans, at the age of six, was best known for giving hugs. His well educated and high achieving parents understandably wanted him to be in an inclusive environment. Han's developmental delays did not stop him from reaching all involved in the special needs ministry. He has recently learned to give handshakes in addition to hugs.

Andy and Henry, now 12 and 14 are brothers with severe epilepsy. Coming from a distance to attend the special needs program, their Mom, a single Mom, going through a painful divorce, said this to me: "it is the only way that we can come to church and is the highlight of our week."

Efrain, a nine year old beautiful child with a profound medically fragile condition, comes to church when he is able. His Mom attends the monthly prayer support group regularly and says that it has given her a new found strength.

Aidan is four and significantly hearing impaired. His parents love the one-on-one volunteer provided for him, as well as the visuals and signing used in the class.

Skyler is 10 years old and has autism with hyperactivity. Being raised by his Grandparents, Skyler and his Grandfather, Dave both attend the special needs class faithfully. While Grandpa Dave does not attend service, he thanks me each week for the lesson taught in Sunday school. And, every week he is asked, in echolalia fashion, by his Grandson, "Did you get that, Dave?"

Kevin is 11. He, too, has autism. His Mom, an attorney, has had to advocate strongly for his rights in the schools and community. At church, we remind her that Kevin is loved and accepted.

Trey was three when his parents brought him to class. Having mild stroke like symptoms and some language delays, he thrived in the consistent and nurturing atmosphere. The family recently moved, and I received a memorable phone call from them. On the other end of the line, Trey's little voice said: "I miss that church."

Margaret was 11 when she decided to come to church with her neighbors, Alex and Raphie, who I mentioned earlier have autism. She ended up being a peer tutor in the class. Her parents soon joined the church, and Margaret's Dad now volunteers with the special needs children regularly.

James was 14 when asked to help as a peer tutor for the class. His parents were long time church members, but had stopped attending. His Mom, a physical therapist was also asked to volunteer in class. The family is back at church.

Andrew, Emily, and Daniel are siblings and peer tutors in the special needs class. Their Mom, a preschool teacher, acts as one of the lead teachers in the special needs program. Their Dad, a musician, plays the guitar and sings every Sunday with this group.

There are many more …and God will continue to send them. Just as He sent volunteers, peers and families with special needs to us, God also provided the resources, materials and curriculum. God will make provisions for your church and the children with disabilities that you will attract.

A teacher and curriculum specialist by trade, I sat in my kitchen late one evening, and wrote up a guide to be used in special needs ministries. Many of the teaching methods that I had used over the years, my studies in curriculum and instruction, my passion for helping all children to become successful learners and my ongoing faith became incorporated into this small book. Inspired by God, I truly believe this is a book that every Sunday school teacher should own. Our special needs ministry began with just a few children in a small space and moved to the church basement the following year. By our fifth year, we had 21 children with disabilities on the roster, 31 peer tutors, and 39 volunteers. In a brand new facility, two reverse inclusion classes –preschool/ primary and intermediate/ middle school are held.   As our children grow, so does the ministry.

With this ministry thriving and a calling from God to keep generating more special needs ministries, my family and I relocated to a second church just down the street from the first. With the blessing and help of the staff here, we would share the special needs mission with another congregation. Following that, forty nine volunteers would come forward. God's power would continue to regenerate a new special needs ministry.

"Sunday school, Sunday school, I want to go to Sunday school." These are the words of class musician, Curtis Repp and I believe the desires of families wishing that church could be a place for them.   With your help and God's it can.

By the grace of God, children and families with disabilities will be saved. God's presence will be felt in your special needs ministries and miracles will happen. God's plan to bring good out of all situations is perhaps His greatest miracle.

My son Zach is now 14. He has endured three neuro surgeries, eighty two different medications, hundreds of clinic appointments and hospitalizations. An air ambulance trip across the country finally confirmed his diagnosis of mitochondrial disease, a rare neuro-degenerative condition. While we do not know his prognosis, in watching him slowly degenerate, our greatest comfort has been in believing that his spirit remains intact. The spirit of God remains generated.

A year ago, folks from Children's Hospital Regional Medical Center and the Make a Wish Foundation visited our home. They asked us if Zach had a wish and if he could tell them his wish. Now completely non-verbal, Zach lay asleep on our downstairs sofa. We thought back to his wishes and requests of us over the years. The memory of him on the swing set returned to my mind. "Mom, will you always help me?" he had asked. "He would like for us to always help him, I said." "He would like to be in his home for a long time," my husband Cal added. With that, they worked to create a fabulous space in our house for Zach. A blank sheet of paper was handed to our then nine year old daughter, Emily. She was told to draw a diagram of how she (and Zach) wanted the room to look, complete with color schemes, furniture, and extra amenities. I nudged my husband and whispered, "Thank the Lord, she has *my* taste."

So, it is as I share with you today, a miracle. In helping my one son to feel God's power, God has enabled others to experience His power as well. My prayer for you is that you will give God the opportunity to turn situations that seem like power failures and darkness into power surges and brightness. With God, despair can be converted to hope. Sorrow can be changed into joy, tragedy into triumph. The special needs ministry is one powerful industry!!! **God's power never dies. His light is always on.**

➡ <u>The Special Needs Mission</u>

"Whoever welcomes one of these children in my name welcomes me."

Mark 9:37

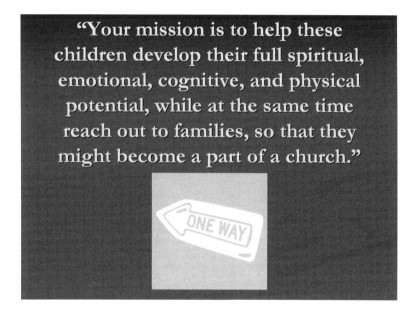

"Your mission is to help these children develop their full spiritual, emotional, cognitive, and physical potential, while at the same time reach out to families, so that they might become a part of a church."

The overall goal of the special needs ministry is to help children and youth with learning, physical, mental and developmental differences and/or health impairments to develop their full spiritual, emotional, cognitive and physical potential, while at the same time reach out to parents and siblings who would like to become part of a church.

Begin the Mission: Give the Gift of Christ

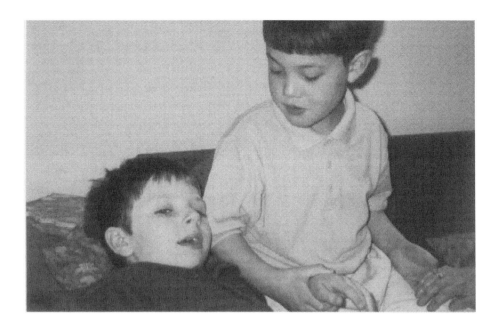

As a former elementary school teacher and curriculum specialist, I've always loved to teach! When I think of teaching Sunday school, I'm reminded that it is like giving a gift…..a gift to ALL children. While it's inevitable that our kids will always want material things and toys, I've come to realize that the greatest gift that we can give to our children is the gift of Christ. This is the gift that will carry them throughout their lives and throughout eternity. I know that's why I've felt led to teach.

Some years ago, when teaching a preschool Sunday class, one of my favorite teachers poked her head into the classroom and said, "It's always a party in here." Teaching Sunday school is a party. In fact, I believe that God sends an invitation to parents and children inviting them to come and celebrate him. He doesn't just invite some kids. He invites ALL of His children. At some churches, He's invited special needs children and their families to participate in a unique children's ministry on Sundays. The dedication of educators, medical professionals, therapists, support persons and parents has truly blessed students with special needs with a collaborative learning opportunity.

 As the mother of a child with significant special needs, it has been both personally and spiritually touching for me to see these kids grow in their faith and their abilities, while at the same time witness parents who have wanted to become part of a church and now have that opportunity.

We want God's invitation to the special needs ministry to reach more families and welcome new students with disabilities as well as typical peers or developmentally appropriate kids to the ministry. We also invite parents and others interested to attend a prayer/support group for families with special needs. Siblings, too, are invited to participate in a support group that's just for them. It's our prayer that people will receive the "invitation" and accept the "gift" to this special ministry or "party" on Sundays.

Many were in church on Palm Sunday when all of the Sunday school children, including the special needs ministry, sang proudly before the congregation. At the conclusion of the song, there was a slight commotion, when one of the kids with special needs darted toward a lit candelabrum.....an adult quickly followed behind, as the boy happily blew out each candle flame. It occurred to me later, that the child had mastered the Sunday school lesson and understood the teaching. After all, he had been invited to a party. He had received the gift of Christ, and now it was time to blow out the candles and celebrate!!!!!!!

Yield to God

The story that I shared with my church years ago, when I first suggested the idea of launching a special needs ministry was this: At the time, my kids were small, and I was feeling very sleep deprived and under a bit of stress. We needed to go someplace in the car, so I got them all bundled up, packed up the trunk, buckled up their belts, locked the doors and began to drive. I kept driving and driving and driving. Finally, I realized that as silly as it seems now, I had actually forgotten where it was that I was going. After awhile, a little voice from the back seat said, "Mommy, where are we going?" There was a silence in our car and after a long pause, I said, "We're going.....home to think about it." I told this story then and now to you, because I feel it's important that we take time to think about where it is that we are going as a church with special needs children. Are we going to welcome in all kids with special needs? Are we going to be a church that is inclusive of all children regardless of their abilities or disabilities? Are we going to be a church that gives all families the opportunity to know God?

I once passed a sign on the road that read "**Those that kneel before God, can stand before anything.**" In many ways, I think that is what inclusive churches allow families with special needs to do. When we place our special children and all of our overwhelming concerns in God's care, we are able to stay strong in His world.

The church special needs ministry is an inclusive ministry. Not only am I the mother of a son, who has significant disabilities and is in a special education program in the school system, I am also the mother of a daughter, who has incredible abilities and is in a gifted education program in the school system. I have often felt that it is my role to advocate for inclusion for a wide spectrum of children.

4

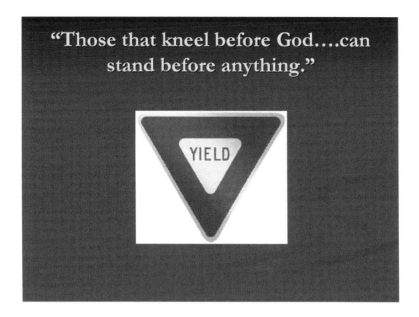

The special needs ministry is a ministry that is highly inclusive, because it INCLUDES ALL CHILDREN. God's doors are open to every child that enters, from those with mild deficits to those with profound disabilities. It is inclusive, because it welcomes in all typically developing children who would like to participate. Finally, it includes many of you as parents, church leaders, staff and volunteers.

Is God calling you to open your heart to special needs children? **Are you ready to ask this question of your church community: Special needs children...who are they and what do they need?**

They are in our community. Some are already in our churches. A good many are at home and would not think of trying church. I ran into a Mom, who shared with me the other day that her son has severe autism. When I broached the topic of church, she quickly said, "My son doesn't do Sunday school. It wouldn't work for him." "You would be surprised," I said "at how well he might do in a program that was specifically tailored for him and others similar to him." I went on to invite her to visit the ministry with her son, so that she could see for herself.

Some years later, I came into contact with an entire school of children who never would have thought that church could be a possibility for them. As our son's condition grew more complex, we enrolled him in a private special education school for high needs students. Here, I would have the opportunity to partner with staff in presenting workshops for the religious community. As a result, more special needs ministries would be inspired and more families would come to know God.

So, who are special needs children and what do they need? They are children first, who simply need a welcome invitation to be included throughout our churches.

As I sometimes say when teaching children with special needs, **"Stop, look and listen," for these families. God will show them to us and enable us to extend the invitation.**

➡️How to Start Out

Remember: Your mission is to help these children to develop their full spiritual, cognitive, emotional, and physical potential, while at the same time reach out to their parents, so that they might become a part of a church.

If you are not already doing so, make a conscious effort to welcome all persons with disabilities into your church as integral members. Perhaps a sign on your church that reads, "We Welcome People with Special Needs," or "Special Needs Ministry Here…" is a good way to begin. Invite a family member of a child with special needs or an adult with disabilities to give a testimonial to your church congregation to promote awareness. Include these individuals and families in all areas of the church.

As you make this mission known, it will not only be children and families with disabilities that you will attract, God will also send volunteers to you. In your church, right now, there are people who are ready to help you with this ministry. They just don't know that you need them, yet. Get ready to ask them.

Go first to your Directors of Children's Ministries or Children's Pastors. Show them this book and tell them what you would like to do. Keep going.

Ask educators: special and regular education teachers, teacher aides, para-educators, instructional assistants, musicians and artists. These people go to your church and they are capable of teaching special children. Phil is a 5th grade teacher at church, who I didn't know. My sister, who had been attending Vacation Bible School with her kids, kept mentioning what a great teacher Phil was. I watched him from a distance at Vacation Bible School. I called him, told him how excellent I thought he was with the VBS children and invited him to be part of the special needs program. In his words, "as a regular classroom teacher, I had little exposure to kids with disabilities. It has opened up a whole new world for me. These children have taught me."

Ask health care professionals. You may not realize it, but you have in your church some people who are physicians, nurses, nurse's aides, technicians and respite care providers. We had a paramedic who had not been involved in church ministries. It turned out; Randy had a gift for working with challenging children who also had medical conditions. He developed a relationship with them and even visited them at home, in his shiny fire truck, I might add, with a couple of his friends.

Ask therapists: physical, occupational, speech and language therapists, psychologists, counselors and behavioral specialists. When they hear that you have a need, they will come forward. At our church,   people who had never taught Sunday school before responded. This was their profession and they realized that they had a gift and a talent to share with us. When we started telling them about these children who needed them, who might not be able to attend church without them, they wanted to help.   Sue and Karen are former physical therapists in clinical settings; Janine is an occupational therapist in a nursing home. Nancy is a speech and language pathologist in the school district. Their knowledge is indispensable in this ministry.

Ask support persons: people who have a heart for these special families and a willingness to learn about their differences. Tim wasn't sure that he would be a good volunteer. A business executive and computer expert, he felt out of touch with children. However, when he passed through the special needs class one day; I noticed how his face lit up when approached by one of the kids. I had to ask three times before he said "yes."   He was our most committed volunteer and was there every single Sunday.

Ask peers. You have a church filled with typical kids who are excellent role models for kids with disabilities. They are role models just by being themselves and they love to get to know kids with special needs. They love to help them. They love to be their friends.   It is a great self esteem building experience for peers, and in turn, the peers learn a lot from the kids with special needs about both compassion and perseverance.

Ask musicians. Every church has musicians and everybody usually knows who they are. Find out if one or two of them can be available to come in weekly to play songs for these kids. Curtis played his guitar and sang songs weekly for the special needs ministry. This was the highlight of the morning for all of the kids and adults. What a gift he gave!

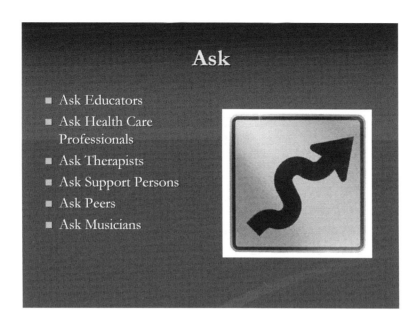

You will also want to ask help for duties outside the classroom, such as **set up, crafts, scheduling/ clerical skills, leadership, prayer support, and siblings support.** (See page 16 for details.)

Next, hold a **training session** for your volunteers and allow them to share their expertise. Make it a collaborative effort. You don't need to do all the work by yourself. This is a church-wide, community ministry. It is a responsibility, I believe. It is an obligation. It is a calling that we all have to help our children…to help God's children. (A separate training for peers works well.)

Inclusion Models

When you have your volunteers, you are ready to **match them 1:1 with students with special needs**. I have used and recommend two different models. The two models compliment one another and do not need to conflict in any way. The first is the "*total inclusion model*" and the second is the *"reverse inclusion model."*

Total Inclusion Model

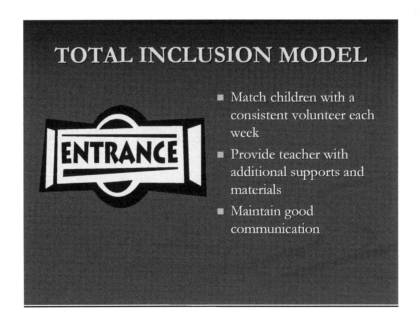

If you have parents that want "*total inclusion*" for their children, then 1:1 volunteers can accompany and guide children through their regular Sunday school experience.   Many children with mild to moderate disabilities and some with significant disabilities at church can be successful in the regular Sunday school classroom, with the assistance of a skilled volunteer. Using the "*total inclusion*" model, I recommend these things:

1. **Try to match these children with a consistent volunteer each week**, so that they are able to develop a rapport with one another and also so that the volunteer learns about and becomes familiar with the child's disability. It is wise to have two people who are trained and aware of the child's needs, so that a substitute is available if needed. A third person could act as a mentor to the student during mid week programs or special events such as Vacation Bible School, Youth Camp or a Holiday play.

2. **Provide the teacher with additional supports and materials.** One suggestion is to have your volunteer carry a bin of helpful aids, things that the child likes and will respond to. Some examples are tactile toys, such as a beanie baby or a textured ball, a communication device for kids that are non-verbal (many kids have language boards at home), sign language cards, pencil grips and specialized scissors for children with fine motor difficulties. Work with the parents and create a kind of a care package that will go with the child each Sunday.

Most important is to maintain good communication between the parent, the Sunday school teacher and the volunteer that is assisting the child.

Communication from Parent to Church:
We often ask parents to communicate with us about their child's needs. To put student folders and parent communication forms into place, see page 163 - 169 "learn from parents." Parents should be encouraged to complete these forms to assist the church in aiding their child.

Communication from Church to Parent:
How are we as a church communicating to parents? Sensitivity is a large part of good communication with parents, due to the emotional elements involved in raising a child with special needs. Put yourself in the place of a parent with a child with special needs. Imagine the courage it takes to begin attending church, not knowing whether your child will be accepted. Consider the irony of the situation. Parents with special needs children need the support of a church, yet finding a church community that embraces their child is not always easy.

Church Communication with Families with Special Needs

The statements below are examples of communications from church to parents of kids with disabilities. Rewrite the following statements to reflect an inclusive church environment.

Following a difficult first day in Sunday school: "Will your child be back next week?"

"Is there a way that you can control your child during service?"

"There's a church in the area that has a great special needs program. Maybe that would work better for your family."

"We're just not sure that we can teach your child."

"We're not really equipped to handle your child's disabilities."

"Not every church is called to begin a special needs ministry."

"We truly don't have the space to accommodate your child. We wish we did."

"We're so short on volunteers. We barely have enough people to cover our Sunday classes, as it is. We're sorry that we aren't able to provide a private volunteer for your child. We hope to be able to in the future."

"It doesn't seem to be working to have your child in the preschool class. Perhaps the nursery would be a better option for her."

"We really love your child, but we need you to accompany him to Sunday school each week. We simply don't have enough help."

Inclusive Church Communication with Families with Special Needs

The statements below are examples of inclusive communications from church to parents of kids with disabilities.

Following a difficult first day in Sunday school: "We hope that your child will be back next week. How can we best support her in the classroom?"

"Is there a way that we can support your child during service? Let's meet to discuss this."

"There's a church in the area that has a great special needs program. Let's look into some of the methods that they are using and try to implement some more effective strategies."

"Please tell us more about your child. What are his likes/ dislikes? What type of learning is he most responsive to? It would be helpful to have you complete a parent questionnaire and provide us with any information that you think would benefit your child and those working with him at church."

"What accommodations and modifications would be most helpful in teaching to your child's disabilities or learning differences?"

"Every church is called to begin a special needs ministry." (Matthew 19:14)

"We are working to creatively accommodate your child's needs."

"We are determined to provide a one on one volunteer for your child so that she can reach her highest potential."

"How are you feeling about having your child in the preschool class? Do you think it would be helpful for him to have a one on one volunteer? Are you open to having him in a special needs reverse inclusion class?"

"We really love your child."

Just as God deals with us as individuals, so should we deal with persons with disabilities as individuals. Provide a progressive special needs ministry that is individualized. Offer both options of total inclusion and reverse inclusion to include all children. This is a ministry that blesses the entire congregation!

Reverse Inclusion Model

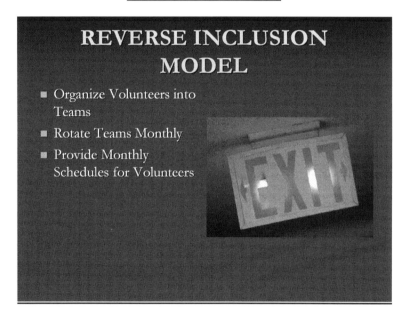

For the "*reverse inclusion model*," I'm going to give you a lot of information. Keep in mind that you can start small and that as your class size increases; you can increase your volunteers. This model works well for kids with significant to profound disabilities, which have great difficulty in a regular classroom setting. However, it could also benefit higher functioning kids, who are in need of an early intervention class. This model can be used in churches of all sizes. (One church of just 50 members uses this approach for their multi-aged Sunday school.) The number of volunteers and students, of course, will vary from church to church.

1. **First, organize your volunteers into teams: lead teachers, medical professionals, therapists, support persons and peer tutors.**
2. **Second, rotate these teams monthly.**
3. **Third, provide monthly schedules for all classroom volunteers that offer a 1:1 teacher-student ratio for the child with special needs (pages 159-161).** You will have an adult, a child with special needs and a "friend" or a "peer." They're a team and they will work together throughout the class. Eventually, you will have lots of teams and they will also work together throughout the Sunday school experience.

→ The Roles of Volunteers and Church Leaders

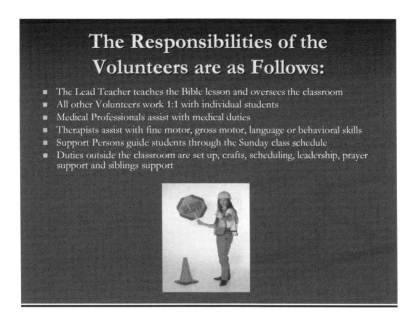

The Responsibilities of the Volunteers are as Follows:

- The Lead Teacher teaches the Bible lesson and oversees the classroom
- All other Volunteers work 1:1 with individual students
- Medical Professionals assist with medical duties
- Therapists assist with fine motor, gross motor, language or behavioral skills
- Support Persons guide students through the Sunday class schedule
- Duties outside the classroom are set up, crafts, scheduling, leadership, prayer support and siblings support

The lead teacher is likely going to be somebody who has done some teaching before and is responsible for teaching the Bible lesson and overseeing the classroom. She or he should model to volunteers how to work with special needs students. This can be achieved through directing teams to specific activities, demonstrating teaching abilities, and guiding and engaging students.

All other volunteers work 1 on 1 with individual students throughout the Sunday, but it is not their responsibility to teach. The lead teacher is not matched with a student, because her responsibility is to oversee and teach.

If possible, and depending on what the needs of your students are, it can be beneficial to have one **medical professional** per class to assist with any medical duties or emergencies. While it's not expected that medical crisis will occur, for kids who have ongoing medical conditions, such as epilepsy, it can be quite a comfort to know that a medical person is nearby.

It is also very helpful to have one or more **therapists** per class. Their role is to assist with gross motor, fine motor, and language or behavioral skills based upon what their specialty is. It is the bringing together of knowledge that creates a successful experience.

Support persons are usually Sunday school teachers, parents, church staff, even pastors who can donate an hour of their time. Many of the volunteers might just volunteer twice a month, so they can be involved in other areas of the church, as well. The job of the support person is to remain with the child, who is being assisted, while guiding him through the Sunday class schedule. This could be in the special needs classes or in the regular classes. Kids participating in the regular program will be more likely to need a consistent volunteer every Sunday due to the fluctuating program. Kids within the "special program" or reverse inclusion program will also need consistency, yet because their program is very consistent, a couple of rotating volunteers per child seems to work fine.

For help outside Sunday mornings, call upon others to assist with the following:

Set Up: Choose one or two people who are orderly and meticulous to set up weekly learning center activities, involving arranging materials, equipment, and supplies.

Crafts: Creative or artistic folks can help with prepping craft materials for art activities.

Administrative Tasks: Those who are clerically minded can aid with scheduling of volunteers, peers and students with special needs.

Prayer Support: When parents feel supported, they are able to act as a strong support for their sons and daughters with disabilities. Select a few people, who are involved in your prayer chain, serve as Stephen Ministers, church deacons, or just have a desire to communicate and pray on a monthly basis with parents about their children's needs, progress, and concerns.

Siblings Support: When parents have a child with special needs, they automatically become a "special needs family." Everyone is affected, including the siblings. Perhaps, your church has an adult sibling of a person with disabilities, a counselor, or someone who has insight on family dynamics. See if these folks can lead a monthly sibling's support group for siblings of special needs students.

Many Children's Hospitals and some schools for kids with disabilities offer "Sibshops," a national program that was founded by Don Meyer, sibling of an adult with special needs and author of Sibshops. Often times, training is provided by these organizations and church volunteers can become certified sibshop leaders. This enables churches to advertise their sibshop, therefore attracting a wider range of families. Sibshops are fun, recreational and supportive of kids with special needs. They are not religious classes, however, these support groups, when held at church, often bring families with disabilities into the church special needs ministry.

Think About who You Have in Your Church

Surely you know of a teacher (preschool, elementary, high school, special education, any type of a teacher) that is in your church.

Are there any medical people that you can recall of off hand in your church?

Are there any therapists in your churches?

Support persons? People who have a heart and willingness to learn about and be with kids with special needs? Who comes to mind right, now?

 A Women's Special Needs monthly prayer support group for Mom's at the church run by three individuals was a Godsend to many.   Judy is a wonderfully dedicated senior who became our "prayer warrior," Heather is a caring church deacon, and Nancy is a compassionate person very committed to and involved with special families. Curtis took a genuine and heartfelt interest in leading the Men's Special Needs group for Dad's.   Can you think of anybody like these people in your church that would make good prayer leaders?

Make a list of folks in your church who are educators, medical persons, therapists, prayer leaders to be contacted about this ministry. If you are unsure as to what qualities people have in your church, make a plan for how you are going to find out (bulletin, church announcement, church office, someone in your church who knows everything about everyone☺). Take a minute now to write down these ideas (page 18).

Did you come up with some names?   Follow up with these individuals or with your plan of recruiting.

 Be sure to pray for God's direction as you invite people to become a part of this ministry. A personal phone call or one on one meeting goes a long way, when it comes to acceptance on the part of the volunteer. Thank people for their participation.   Provide encouragement for those who are considering becoming involved and keep a running list of those who may be interested at a later time.

 During your recruitment, some may ask: **"How should I treat persons with disabilities?" The answer is this...like Jesus did.** Throughout the Bible, Jesus encounters persons that we might say today have "special needs." What did Jesus do in these situations?

1. He opened his heart to them by making eye contact, touching them physically and spiritually, calling them by name.
2. He treated them as individuals by involving them in plans, asking what they wanted, and listening to and watching for their responses.
3. He was sensitive to them and their families by helping with their needs and praying for them. We can welcome families with special needs by responding to them just as Jesus.

WHO WIL YOU ASK TO JOIN YOU IN THE SPECIAL NEEDS MINISTRY?

Ask Educators-

_____
_____
_____

Ask Health Care Professionals-

_____
_____
_____

Ask Therapists-

_____
_____
_____

Ask Support Persons-

_____
_____
_____

Ask Musicians-

_____
_____
_____

Ask Peers-

_____
_____
_____

Ask Prayer Leaders and Siblings Group Leaders-

_____
_____
_____

If you are unsure about what backgrounds or qualities people in your church have, make a plan for how you will find out.

_____
_____
_____

When You Need More Volunteers....

What should you do if you have asked, yet still don't have the number of volunteers needed to provide a safe and successful ministry?

1. Work together with church staff so that you can coordinate ministry needs.

2. Check the church database for congregant backgrounds and interests (educators, therapists, health care, support, prayer). Assess spiritual gifts of volunteers that would compliment the ministry.

3. Publicize your needs through church bulletins, e-mails, announcements and testimonials made during worship services.

4. Invite prospective volunteers to an informational meeting. Allow families with special needs and current volunteers to share about the blessing of being involved in the ministry.

5. Utilize people and groups who are not heavily involved in the church. For example, seniors might prep craft materials or help to lead a prayer group. Sometimes members of the church who haven't found their "niche" fit in nicely within the special needs ministry.

6. Ask a volunteer to help with recruiting other volunteers.

7. Check in with parents of children with special needs on the dates that they plan to attend church. While, of course last minute changes occur, most families know if/ when they are going to be out of town for holidays and family events.

8. Re-ask those who have said, "no" by prefacing the great need and that God has brought their name to you again.

9. Ask those who have already committed to consider increasing their volunteer time.

10. Ask folks in the community who have an interest in Special Education but are not necessarily "church goers." It's a great way to introduce them to the church. (Be sure to have all volunteers, especially those who are new, complete safety background checks in compliance with your denomination regulations.)

11. Pray and ask others to join you in prayer.

How to Match Volunteer with Student

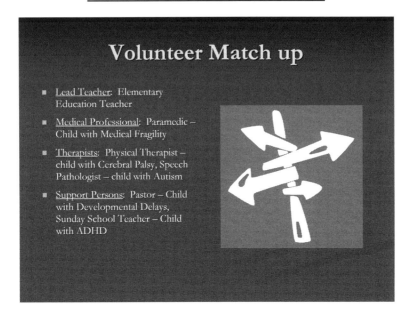

When matching a special student with a volunteer, carefully consider the volunteers background and experience. Look closely at the strengths and weaknesses of each child.

Above is an example of a volunteer match up with students with special needs. A lead teacher might be an elementary school teacher. A medical professional could be a paramedic matched with a student with medical fragility. A therapist could be a physical therapist matched with a child with cerebral palsy. A speech pathologist might work well with a child with autism. A support person, such as a pastor, could be matched with a child with developmental delays, a Sunday school teacher with a child with (ADHD) attention deficit with hyperactivity disorder.

Student Placement in the Special Needs Program

I am sometimes asked how to determine placement of special students within church school. For some this can be a controversial issue. In the years that I have been involved in the special needs ministry, I have never allowed myself to get into a disagreement with a team member over student placement or program of a student. This is due to the fact that I don't believe this decision is mine to make. I consider parents the true experts on their own children.

Studies show that 90% of the time parents are "right." This is not to say that I have always been in agreement with parent requests. In the past, I have tactfully made constructive suggestions to parents on the placement of their children and witnessed these scenarios:

1.) The parent was right about placement and the child was successful in the placement the parent requested.
2.) The parent was wrong about placement but in time changed their mind so that their child could be successful.

In cases where students are not placed in "my ideal" situation for them, I have tried to provide as many supports as possible and to coordinate and communicate well with the classroom or youth program leaders. I have kept an honest and sincere dialogue going with parents so that they might feel open to change. I have prayed for and asked for additional prayer for these parents.

While, I have not ever had a team member come to me directly and tell me specifically that they "are in disagreement with a student placement or program," should this happen, I would be appreciative of their input and ask them to detail their concerns for me before the parent, a special needs steering committee and/ or pastor. Together, we would make the best choice for the child and family. Careful consideration would be given to safety issues, extreme classroom disruption and strong parental feelings. I am in favor of putting the needs of the child first and at the same time taking into account the effect that the decision will have on the family as a whole. There are many barriers that prevent parents of special children from becoming Christians. The special needs ministry can break down these barriers by responding with sensitivity and care.

The Steering Committee

Set up a steering committee or leadership team to pray for, plan for and guide your ministry. The committee can consist of the Director of Children's Ministries, Special Needs Coordinator/Director (if your church has already appointed one), some knowledgeable educators and several parents of special needs students. The committee may help implement many of the guidelines addressed in this book, as well as, devise some protocol or policies that apply specifically to your own church.

This team may also plan for special events such as community outreaches for those with disabilities. This might include holiday gatherings or parties, outings that the ministry would like to sponsor, volunteer respite for parents, disability awareness meetings or workshops, and providing resources through a special needs ministry newspaper.

Other subjects for discussion include: selecting and planning curriculum, creating a cohesive learning atmosphere, keeping God's church doors open to all children with disabilities, following up with and ministering with special families throughout the week, helping the challenging child to be successful in the Sunday school classroom, respecting issues of confidentiality, enlisting and maintaining the help of volunteers, training volunteers and peer helpers and staying informed about Christian special education. Most importantly, the special needs steering committee should make sure that the overall mission or philosophy is carried throughout the classroom and ministry.

The Director of Special Needs Ministries

When your ministry is in place and your church is ready to fully support it, select a director or coordinator of special needs ministries. This person will have a love for Christ and His special children, as well as, strong, organizational and leadership skills. Formal teaching experience and much knowledge about learning, physical, mental and social differences are desirable. (The teaching, administrative and ministering duties of the special needs director are described on pages 25-27.)

The Children and the Church

Most churches want very much to welcome children with disabilities, but often aren't sure how to accommodate their needs. Setting up a special needs ministry allows the church to reach out to and embrace these children and their families in their times of trials. It allows special families to let God guide and carry them through their daily difficulties. When the church adopts the idea that they will put a special needs ministry in place, they will be amazed by the children that God will send to them.

The Volunteers

In your church right now, there are skillful and compassionate people that will come forward when they know that there is a need. Whether you are beginning with just one special needs child or a number of children, seek out and personally invite others to join you in this ministry.

Coming Soon: <u>Special Needs Ministry</u>
<u>Ministers to Children with Special Needs and their Families</u>

This exciting ministry serves children/ youth with special needs and their families by providing unique Sunday classes.
The Sunday school classes:
- Serve preschool, elementary school, and secondary school aged kids with learning, physical, mental and developmental differences and/or health impairments
- Offer a student/teacher ratio of 1:1
- Provide reversed inclusion with typical peers in "special" classrooms
- Provide total inclusion in regular classrooms
- Are taught in small groups at theme based "hands-on" activity centers
- Include a structured learning environment with individualized learning instruction

Volunteer staff consists of:
- Educators
- Medical professionals
- Physical, occupational, and speech therapists
- Trained support staff
- A musician

For some families, this is the first opportunity they've had to attend church services. A monthly prayer/support group for special parents is also offered as well as a monthly support group for siblings.

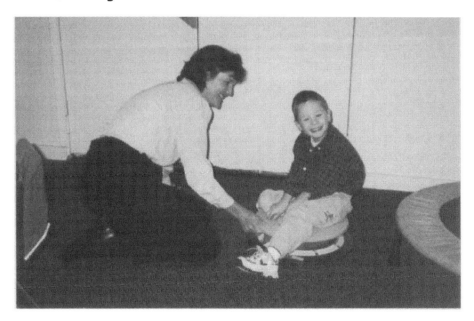

Permission to photocopy this handout granted for local church use.
© 2007 Amy Rapada

The Role of Director of Special Needs Ministries

The overall goal of the special needs ministry is: to help children and youth with learning, physical, mental, and developmental differences and/or health impairments to develop their full spiritual, cognitive, emotional and physical potential, while at the same time reach out to parents and siblings who would like to become part of a church.

Teaching Responsibilities:

- Oversee or teach the weekly special needs Sunday school class or classes.

- Develop and implement curriculum for preschool, elementary and secondary children with varying degrees of disabilities ranging from mild to severe.

- Work closely with the director of children's ministries, youth director, educators, health care professionals, therapists and support persons to create a collaborative learning opportunity for children with disabilities.

- Communicate weekly with volunteers to discuss children's needs, progress, and concerns.

- Provide workshops and training sessions for classroom volunteers.

- Train "peer tutors" or developmentally appropriate children to work successfully with students with special needs.

- Plan and coordinate special needs events (eg. Christmas, and Easter gatherings) and assist director of children's ministries and youth director with some integration during other church events.

Administrative Responsibilities:

- Recruit and maintain a large number of classroom volunteers who have experience in special education, related fields or an interest in being trained.

- Enlist the help of peer tutors.

- Register individual students with special needs, which involves meeting with parents to discuss their child's needs, interests and abilities.

- Provide monthly schedules for all classroom volunteers that offer a 1:1 teacher student ratio.

- Follow and periodically update a "special needs class" handbook. The handbook should include a mission statement; the responsibilities of volunteers, a parent questionnaire, a lesson plan outline, medication release form, and other instructions.

- Maintain individual confidential files for special students to be used by teachers to benefit the child in the classroom.
- Record and file teaching lesson plans and sample projects used in the classroom.
- Distribute, collect and respond to yearly class evaluations.

Ongoing Ministering:

- Communicate and pray on a weekly basis with parents about their children's needs, progress, and concerns.

  Develop a rapport with special families and an understanding of their child's differences.
- Lead or participate in a monthly prayer support group for special needs families and friends.
- Share with the church and advertise to the community about the special needs class and other special needs events.

Responsibilities of Special Needs Volunteers

Here are some guidelines for becoming an effective volunteer:

A.   Be prepared

- Arrive 15 minutes early to familiarize yourself with the child that you are paired with. Check the "teacher/student partnership board and special needs files to read information about the child that you are assisting.

- Read the classroom safety guidelines.

- Be sure to know if your child can use the bathroom or has to be changed, and whether they should be changed during class.

- Know where supplies, materials and equipment are located.

- Communicate with teachers and other volunteers. Share ideas of expertise. Remember, this is a collaborative effort!

- Offer a prayer up each week, with your fellow volunteers to ensure that God is at the center of your ministry.

B.   Make the class meaningful

- Aim to help all children have a successful learning experience. Focus on the special child's abilities but develop an understanding of the child's disabilities. Work to maintain a great rapport with children and help them to meet their goals.

- Encourage friendships and train peer tutors to work side by side with students with special needs. Emphasize to peers that their job is to "be themselves" and in doing so they will be acting as role models to the children with special needs. Peers will also learn a great deal about perseverance and compassion from the kids with special needs.

- Introduce the Bible verse: "I have made you wonderfully." (Psalms 119) Discuss the ways in which God has made each of us to be unique. Years ago, when teaching kindergarteners a lesson on multicultural diversity, my students were excited to share their uniqueness. One student told about being Asian American, another African American. One raised his hand and said with confidence, "I'm tri-cities." While he may not have used the correct ethnic terminology, he was proud to be who he was. Create a celebration of diversity amongst your students with and without special needs. Encourage them to be proud of who they are and who God is shaping them to become.

⬥How to Choose and Adapt a Curriculum for Students with Special Needs

Children with disabilities are *not* disabled children. There is so much that they *are* able to do (if they have supportive and loving people to enable them)!! In his book Exceptional Teaching, Jim Pierson **says: "Of course, children with disabilities can learn, the real question is can we teach?"** I say "yes" if we have two things: **knowledge and compassion.**

Many of you have children with disabilities coming into churches and if you don't, it is likely because they are home and think that they can't be successful at Sunday school. We want them to know that they can. We want to help kids with special needs really learn at church.

*Appropriate curriculum brings out the abilities or strengths in students. Select a curriculum that is comprised of:

- Age appropriate skills (if your class has a range of ages, choose a curriculum that is mid-line and supplement with both higher and lower level materials.)
- Large, colorful visuals
- Predictable stories that have a pattern
- Narrative text or expository text with basic concepts for younger students and more complex concepts for older students
- Stories that incorporate music

- Affirmations and Bible verses
- Opportunities for active participation
- Clear, concise points
- Some repetition of facts
- Smooth transitions
- Props/objects, puppets, costumes

* Inappropriate curriculum brings out the disabilities or weaknesses in students

Avoid curriculum that is:

- Not age appropriate
- Very wordy
- Overly stimulating
- Didactic verses interactive
- Socially advanced or non-applicable to students
- Unpredictable or unclear

.

Recommended Christian Curriculum for Special Needs Students:

- *Group Hands on Curriculum* by Group Publishing, Inc.
  toddler/preschool–grade 6
- *Gospel Light Curriculum* by Gospel Light, Publishing, Inc.
  toddler/preschool–grade 6
  Kingdom Kids Curriculum by Kingdom Publishers
  toddler/preschool–grade 6
- *Old and New Testament Felt Stories* by Betty Lukens
  teacher's manual written for and used in mission fields
  all ages
- *Read Aloud Bible Stories* by Helen Lindvall
  toddler–grade 1
- *Read Aloud Parables* by Helen Lindvall
  toddler–grade 1
- *Word and Song Bible Stories* by Max Lucado, Joni Eareckson Tada, Steve Green, Adrian Rogers and others
  ages 3-10
- *Arch Book Series* by Concordia Publishing House
  ages 5-9
- *Religious Education Lessons for the Disabled* by the Archdiocese of Seattle
  grades 1-12
- *Friendship Ministries: Bible Studies, Take Home Papers, Life Studies by Barbara Newman, Jessie Schut and others*
  ages 10-20
- *Disability Ministry Sunday Kit by Joni and Friends*
  all ages

<u>**Supplementary Materials:**</u>

- *The Pray and Play Bible* by Group Publishing, Inc. preschool-grade 1
- *The Pray and Play Bible 2* by Group Publishing, Inc. preschool-grade 1
- *Felt Play Storybooks* by Standard Publishing, Inc. ages 4-10
- *Read With Me Bible Stories for First Readers* by Abingdon Press, ages 5-6
- *A Picture That! Story Bible* by Zonderkidz ages 4-8
- *Adam, Adam* by Bill Martin, Jr. ages 3-8
- *The Eager Reader Bible* by Tyndale Kids ages 2-8
- *NIV Young Discoverer's Holy Bible* by Zonderkidz ages 6-12
- *Holy Bible New King James Version* by Nelson Bibles for kids ages 8-12

<u>**Teaching Tools:**</u>

- **PECS** (Picture Exchange Communication System) Boardmaker software program by Mayer and Johnson
- **Writing with Symbols** Communication System by Mayer and Johnson
- **Communication Devices** – "The BIG MAC" button, "Go Talk" device and many others by Ablenet
- **Sign Language Computerized Program** by Martin Sternberg
- **Abilitations Catalog** for ordering materials for students with special needs
- **Integrations Catalog** for ordering materials for students with sensory integration difficulties
- **Sportstime Catalog** for ordering materials and equipment for those with physical challenges
- **Lakeshore Learning Catalog** for ordering materials for students with learning disabilities

<u>**How to Adapt Curriculum to Fit the Needs of Special Learners**</u>

Assess the needs of your students

Some of the common deficits noted in kids with disabilities are difficulties with:
- Processing information
- Making transitions
- Understanding social boundaries
- Sensory integration
- Motor control
- Hearing and vision
- Speech and language production
- Attention and impulsivity
- Health issues

*processing information- taking in knowledge, breaking it down into understandable parts can be challenging. We need to allow kids ample time to process directions and to respond to those directions. We can also simplify and shorten our instructions. We can give one and two step commands. We can

alter our vocabulary depending upon the specific disability of the child that we are working with.

making transitions- changing from one activity to the next is sometimes problematic for kids. So, we need to use clear and smooth transitions. I offer these examples: "stop, look and listen," "Be ready for the music it's time to clean up our room," "be thinking about moving to the next activity," or "one more minute, one more minute to play, one more minute, until we put our toys away." Signs and songs that give kids an early warning help them to transition.

understanding social boundaries- knowing how to be socially appropriate is something we take for granted. For kids who have "social thinking deficits," though, these skills need to be taught. Even a simple greeting can be awkward for a child who lacks the understanding of social boundaries. We can help this child by saying, can you say, "hello teacher" or "hello friend."   One of the traits that I love about children with autism is that they often use echolalia or a form of echoing what they've heard. If I say "Good Morning Raphie," he might cheerfully say back, "Good Morning, Raphie." I usually say, "I'm glad you told yourself to have a good morning. Now say, Good Morning, Amy" or "Good Morning Teacher." We can validate children and then teach them to understand social situations.

Sometimes children with social deficits will unknowingly say things that are unkind and hurtful. However, we have the ability to help them, and so do the non disabled kids who work along side them. I know a child with Asperger's syndrome, which is a high functioning form of autism, who once said to a non disabled peer, "I just have to tell you that I hate those boots that you're wearing." The peer looked at him and said, "Well, I could say that I don't like your poke' man socks, but that wouldn't be very polite."   Instead I'll just say, "Have a nice day." We can teach kids to say appropriate things by our example.

sensory integration- trouble integrating all of the five senses, is for many children with disabilities, the main factor that makes learning in a busy classroom almost impossible. It's impossible unless…we are able to create an atmosphere that encourages the development of the senses. We can create an environment that gives children opportunities to utilize all of their senses…their seeing, their hearing, their touching, their tasting and their smelling. We want to use all five senses to target sensory integration dysfunction.

motor control- weakness with muscles, large and small and motor planning issues are common for kids with disabilities. We need to provide these children with help of fine motor and gross motor skills.   You may not realize that you have in your churches, occupational and physical therapists who would like to help. If they are called upon to share their gifts with these special children, my guess is that they will do just that.

hearing and vision – impairments of sound and sight can cause a lot of confusion for students in a fast paced classroom. We can always use lots of visuals, signing, clear oral   directions, Children's Braille books, books on tape, and close proximity to guide these students through their Sunday experience.

*speech and language production- communication disorders are extremely varied. They can range from kids who have simple articulation problems to kids with limited speech or language delays to children who are totally non-verbal. We can provide these children with a rich language experience by immersing them in a classroom filled with print, spoken words, pictures, signing and communication devices. Look for the speech and language pathologist at your church. There is probably one. Ours has been with us for five years and has been able to set up some modes of communication for students who have diverse needs.

*attention and impulsivity- issues with hyperactivity and impulsive behaviors can make the Sunday school classroom an oppositional place to be. These children have an innate tendency to be very active. We want to meet their needs and allow them to be active, by setting up appropriate places and equipment for them to release their energy. When they are allowed to jump on a mini trampoline, ride an exercise bike or crawl through a play tunnel during "center time" or "settling in" time at the beginning of class, they are usually able to focus more during the lesson portion of class.

*health issues- compromised health is common in kids with disabilities. We should offer safety (including safety plans for individual students), comfort, and a calm and organized environment. Tap into the minds of the health care professionals in your church and get them involved in your ministry.

Begin by choosing a curriculum that is adaptable. Most curriculums can be adapted to fit the needs of special education students. However, some curriculum is better suited than others. (Avoid curriculum that has the characteristics listed on page 31.)

Align the curriculum to fit the needs of the students

- **List the abilities and strengths of the students**
I want you to think, for just a moment, about some of the kids that you know with disabilities. *Close your eyes right now.* If you are a parent, your own child will naturally come to mind. Choose one child, in particular to focus on. When you think of this child, do you think of the things that he or she *cannot* do? Do you think of this child's deficits first? I want you to change your thinking and think instead of the things that this child *can* do. *Open your eyes now*. Think of this child's capabilities and jot them down on a piece of paper at this time. **Write down all of the strengths that you see in this individual. (See workspace page 36).**

Students may range greatly in their abilities. Some students may be highly verbal and gifted readers. Others might sign, gesture or use communication devices. Some children may be quite attentive and demonstrate the ability to sit appropriately. Some may be able to maintain joint attention and social interaction. Take note of the child's senses that are intact. Can the student see, hear, feel, taste and smell? Focus on and use this range of abilities to teach new skills.

- **List the strengths and weaknesses of the curriculum**

Now, turn your thoughts to a curriculum that you have at your church. Think of a Sunday school program that you are either using as a teacher, supporting if you are a church leader or observing as a parishioner or parent. **Write down one strength that you like about your curriculum that works well with this child. Then write down one weakness of the curriculum that you dislike and don't think works well with this child.**

Match the traits with the students' capabilities. For instance, a curriculum that has too few visuals needs to be supplemented with posters, pictures, a felt board or other aides.   Lessons that have too much "teacher talk" should be shortened and replaced with more student involvement. In a curriculum where affirmations and Bible verses are used, these can be emphasized. If a lesson is too stimulating for students, certain activities or questions may need to be eliminated. A soft tone and peaceful background music can also be added to create a calmer environment. If curriculum is not engaging to students, many props/objects and creative dramatics must be used to hold their attention. Simple sign language and communication devices may be added to accommodate learning differences.

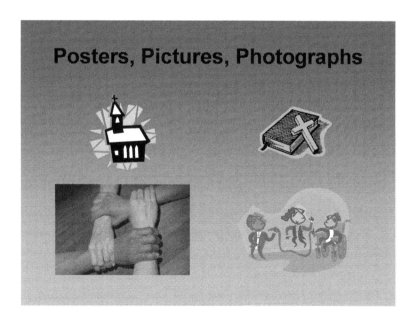

"Align the Curriculum to Fit the Student's Needs" Workspace

*List the abilities and strengths of the student:

_____
_____
_____
_____
_____
_____
_____
_____
_____
_____
_____
_____

*List the strengths and weaknesses of the curriculum:

_____
_____
_____
_____
_____
_____
_____
_____
_____
_____
_____
_____

*Match the curriculum traits with the student's capabilities:

_____
_____
_____
_____
_____
_____
_____
_____
_____
_____
_____

Align "Life of the Church" Curriculum to fit the Student's Needs

*Put necessary student accommodations/ modifications in place

1. Provide mentors for younger children and/ or peer buddies for older children during "life of the church" opportunities:

 -worship service participation
- receiving of communion
-religious classes
- mid week programs
-special events

2. Give mentors or peer buddies helpful materials and equipment to help meet student needs. See page 11 for teacher supports/ materials.

-tactile toys or fidgets for those with distractibility during services or class
- communication devices/ sign language cards for kids with non-verbalism or limited speech (many kids have language boards at home)
-pencil grips, specialized scissors and crayons for children with fine motor difficulties
-specialized chairs or appropriate seating for those with physical challenges

3. Be sure that your church building is in compliance with the American Disabilities Act and that physical access is available to all

4. Encourage full participation in "life of the church" worship opportunities:

-families with special needs are seated in the front or back of the service if requested
-families with special needs receive communion first to avoid wait time
-communion sacraments are brought to a family with special needs during service if requested
-communion sacraments are brought to a child during special needs class if requested
-religious class materials are modified to meet the needs of the student

*Prepare the student for the experience

-Visit the church sanctuary, building for worship, or classroom with the student before services or events take place
- Familiarize students to worship hymns or praise songs before services or special programs
-Expose students to church liturgy or religious practices
-Read and practice church scripture at home
-Listen to a tape recorded or online version of the sermon and communion wording at home
-Meet with your Pastor or Minister for preparatory classes and/ or to practice communion
-Meet with your Pastor, Minister or church leader before participating in a mid week or special program activity
-Attend practices or rehearsals for special events or church programs

→How to Involve Students with Special Needs in the Learning Process

When we have adapted curriculum or chosen one that fits the needs of our students, we should **actively involve students in the learning process.** This helps them to stay engaged in the teaching and on task during the lesson.

For instance in the Biblical story of "Jesus Blesses the Children," we can ask kids to participate like this. To a reader, we might ask that he read a Bible verse. "*Let's read: Suffer little children... to come unto me.*" *Matthew 19:14.* To a child with speech limitations, we can ask that she repeat a phrase. "*Say, Jesus loves all children.*" To a child with non-verbalism, we can ask that he touch, or point to, or put a felt piece of Jesus on a storyboard. "*Raise your hands to Jesus, now.*" For a child with physical challenges, we can bring the story board or book to him and use hand over hand guidance to prompt him. A child with hearing impairments can sign, "Jesus." "*Please sign Jesus with us, everyone.*" Kids can help turn pages and act out situations. When Jesus turns to His disciples in Matthew chapters 18 and 19 and says "Do not send the children away; I invite all children to come to Me," kids can practice these lines. Continue throughout your lessons to involve the students.

The National Education Association on Developmentally Appropriate Practices cites that **"Learning is something that kids do not something that is done to them."** I would add to that by saying: *Let the children do the things that they can do. There is something that every child can do.*

38

Focus on Kids' Strengths Versus their Weaknesses

One Sunday, I was teaching a lesson on God's Promise to Abraham and Sarah to bless them with the child that they had prayed for...who they would one day name Isaac.   I had asked many of the children to participate, using all of the methods that I have described to you—reading, repeating phrases, signing, gesturing, holding a prop or touching a picture. There was one child who was visiting our class for the first time, who had very profound disabilities. I was not sure that he was able to do any of the things that I had asked so far of the other children.

As I continued teaching, I prayed at the same time that God would show me this child's strength. Just as I was getting to the conclusion of the Bible story, this child let out a loud, happy squeal. Miraculously, the last sentence that I read aloud said, "the Biblical meaning of the word Isaac is laughter." I was then able to turn to this child, in front of the entire class, and say "thank you for teaching us this important fact." The presence of God's Spirit will be not only within you but within the blessed children that you are teaching.

Grouping Students

Although it may be tempting to divide students based on their developmental abilities within the special needs ministry, this is not appropriate education. Appropriate practice allows students to learn from others who are different from themselves. In other words, the diversity of the classroom makeup can stimulate learning opportunities. For example, non-verbal children learn speech from those who speak; children, who lack social skills, learn socialability from those who are interactive.

If it is necessary to divide children due to a large class size, do so chronologically. To ensure a sense of respect for the child with special needs and her family, be consistent with the decided age division. This gives every child the opportunity to benefit from peers her own age.

Never assume the receptive abilities of any child. Instead, teach children everything they seem capable of learning within the limits of their conditions. All children, when provided with appropriate Christian curriculum, specific methods, and God's ever presence can be successful learners in the special needs ministry mission.

→How to Create a Successful Experience for Students with Special Needs

The next step is to put a new class structure and lesson format into place. In creating this learning experience, we want to provide an educational and a spiritual based program. **Successful learners...Enabled learners that is what we want.** Because the children with disabilities and the typical peers in your classroom have diverse needs, **a consistent yet differentiated structure needs to be in place.**

This is a consistent structure, but the activities are changed weekly and accommodate for differentiated instruction. Kids work at their own level at these stations. It is a structure that has been found to be very effective in helping kids with disabilities to grow and progress in their abilities.

Again, keep in mind that the aim of the special needs ministry is to provide an atmosphere where all students can be successful, regardless of their abilities or disabilities. We want for this one hour on Sundays to be a positive experience for children and adults. This particular **class structure**, I believe will enable that to happen. This Sunday class schedule (page 51) is a format that can be used in the special needs classroom with reverse inclusion as well as in the regular Sunday classroom. If you can put something like this into place, kids will do well, because it's a predictable schedule that they can follow. The activities, though, are always varied and always fun.

Take on the challenge of creating one new activity or learning center that is specifically tailored for special needs students. A learning center is a well defined workspace for children to learn using hands on materials. This is how you can begin your Sunday mornings. It is a "settling in" time. Often, kids with disabilities have a difficult time transitioning from home to church. Center time peaks their interest immediately and allows them to make wise choices. Because these children come to us with diverse types of needs, centers are also a way to tap into a range of deficits.

At your church, you may want to have a **book corner**, also called a cozy or cuddly corner. It is a comfy space filled with cushions, a blanket and books to go along with the lesson. This is a comforting and soothing area. While it's appealing to many children, it works especially well for those with profound or medically fragile conditions. These kids enjoy listening to a story told by an adult or a peer.

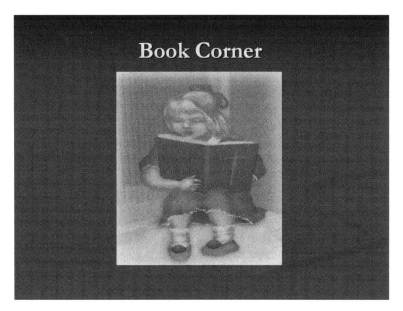

Suggestions for Books to Begin With:

Accept and Value Each Person by Cheri J. Meiners
A First Look at the Bible by Lois Rock
Blossom (for girls) New Testament Magazine by Nelson Bibles
Explore (for boys) New Testament Magazine by Nelson Bibles
God Knows Me! by Joel Anderson
I Can Pray with Jesus by Debbie Trafton O'Neal
Kids Say "Thank You God!" by Andy Robb
Let's Talk About Heaven by Debby Anderson
Boys and Girls Life Application Study Bibles – New Living Translations
My Devotions- Braille Editions by The Lutheran Library for the Blind
Poems and Prayers for Children by Publications International Ltd.
Prayer for a Child by Rachel Field
Reach Out and Give by Cheri J. Meiners

You may have a **sensory center**, which is a table or tub to be filled with a tactile substance, such as rice, beans, water, etc. Many children with disabilities have sensory integration dysfunction. This lets them get some sensory input that they crave.

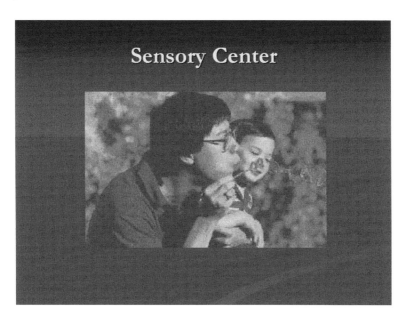

The **fine motor center** is a small muscle center with puzzles, manipulatives, building activities, paper pencil tasks, etc. For kids with motor planning issues and physical limitations, this station provides great practice. With the Assistance of a volunteer, children can complete hand over hand tasks.

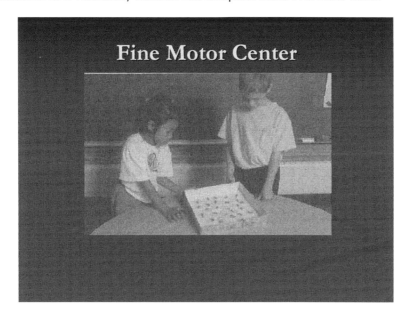

The **gross motor center** is a large muscle center: a mini trampoline, crawling tunnel, a therapy ball, a sensory disc, think BIG! Children with some physical challenges or children with attention deficits can benefit greatly from this opportunity. It's a chance to release energy. (Teachers may benefit from it, too). ☺

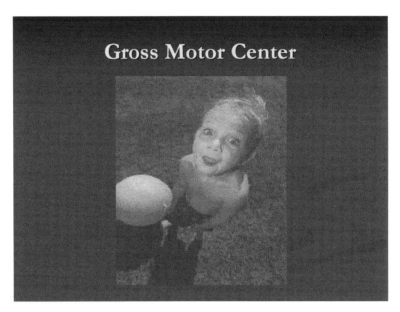

The **art center** includes a multitude of craft supplies, crayons, paints, paper, collage materials, etc. This is a tremendous outlet for all children and a wonderful way for kids with non-verbalism and kids with behavioral/ emotional disorders to express themselves.

Other suggestions are a **writing center**, a **game center** and a **music center.** The types of all of these centers remain the same throughout the year. However, the activities at the centers are changed weekly or monthly to coordinate with the lessons.

I'm giving you the challenge of creating just one center so that you are not overwhelmed. I want you to start small. Choose the center that you feel your students are most in need of. All of your students, however, will learn from this activity. It might provide some down time or variety. Come up with some supplies to put in that center. My hope is that you can set this up at your church right away.

In time, you will be able to set up additional, simultaneous centers for your students. Some kids may choose to stay at one center for half an hour, some might move through each center, rapidly. I know one student, who uses the therapy ball, as an incentive to move from center to center. The completion of one activity entitles him to 50 bounces on the big ball. (Just about everyone in his class learns to count to at least 50! ☺)

Finally, the last factor of the class structure is the **classroom arrangement or the adaptation of the classroom environment.**

Page 46 illustrates an example of classroom set up. It shows how centers can be placed throughout the room. It also gives an idea of how to create a separate lesson area. However you choose to set up your classroom, it is crucial that the room be arranged in a similar way each Sunday to provide familiarity and routine for kids who need predictability in order to function.

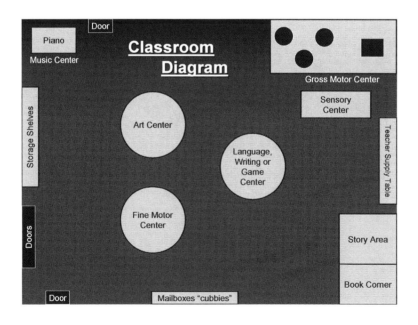

As you look over the classroom diagram of seven centers, keep in mind that this is an ideal proposal, a ministry at its very best! Realistically, I'm guessing that you are probably thinking, "but, we're in a small space and it's a shared space." Sound familiar? Are you in that situation? We were, as well. In fact, when our class began 7 years ago, we were in a very small room. When I looked at it closely, though, I saw four corners, which meant four learning centers, one in each corner. The center of the room was used for story or Bible time followed by craft time, on a table behind our story mat.

To solve the dilemma of shared space, we brought in bins and organized all of our materials so that they could be quickly stacked and cleaned up. By setting out a large "clean up" container, students were able to put things in to help. A storage space is also a plus, if you have one available. By all means, do not let space stop you from beginning a special needs ministry.

I was fortunate at both churches that my family and I attended to have Children's Pastors who shared my vision for a special needs ministry. In consulting with and presenting to many churches over the years, I have discovered that this is not always the case.

Louise Tucker Jones, an author of special ministries, tells of beginning a ministry for a couple of students with disabilities in a storage closet. Fortunately, the church eventually recognized that her closet sized ministry was growing and soon placed the group in a regular sized classroom. Certainly, I'm not suggesting that you begin in a closet, but what I am saying is to look at your space with an open mind. Think of it as a temporary space, one that may grow in time as your ministry grows along with the growth and understanding of others. When you have taken on this attitude of patience, your physical space will fall into order.

Likewise, this is also the attitude that should be taken when it comes to requesting financial support to begin a special needs ministry. I am frequently asked how much it costs to support a ministry like this...with specialized gross motor equipment, fine motor manipulatives, tactile craft supplies, sensory toys, and curriculum related materials. The answer is this: Not as much as one would imagine.

Make a list of the items that you will need for your learning centers (See pages 55-56 and see "special needs wish list" on page 49).   Publicly share this list with your church and ask for donations first. You will be surprised to find how many folks have an exercise bike or a mini trampoline sitting in their garage that they are glad to get rid of. The same is true for children's puzzles, books, games, building activities, music CD.'s/ tapes, cushions/ pillows, etc.

Next, refer to the list of curriculum and teaching tools on pages 31-32. If your curriculum is adaptable (Most curriculum is...), add the necessary accommodations and modifications to your current curriculum to meet the special population that you have or that you expect to have.

Take a look through some good learning or special education catalogs and circle the needed materials and supplies (See page 32 for a list of catalogs.) You may choose to purchase your top priorities through these sources, but be sure to visit your local more economical stores first.

 Target usually offers great puzzles, building and learning manipulatives.   Fred Meyers often has excellent sensory toys and large bins that can be used for sensory tubs. IKEA, most of the time, sells play tunnels and some sensory appropriate furniture, such as fuzzy bean bag chairs and hammocks. Local drugstores, such as Bartell Drugs and Rite Aid sometimes carry tactile balls (such as "gak splat," " koosh", "crush," "inside-out" "spaghetti," "worm," "water," and "stress" balls).   Tactile rubberized (world creature "stretchable") animals and small nylon pillows are sold as well at gift and bed and bath stores.

Special Needs Ministry Wish List

Our special needs ministry is starting from scratch. Any of the following items that you can donate from home or purchase would be much appreciated:

- Cushions and pillows (large and soft)
-Fleece blankets
-Children's Christian books (preschool-youth age level)
-DVD player or tape recorder
-Sturdy storage bins with lids (all sizes)
- puzzles (wooden framed, jigsaw, and foam, various levels of difficulty)
- Building activities (legos, duplos, Lincoln logs, wooden blocks, waffle blocks, lacing cards, stringing beads, pegboards, tinker toys, sorting toys etc.)
-Games (board, electronic, and card, various levels of difficulty)
- Mini trampoline
- Therapy or Pilate's balls
- Play tunnel
-Sensory discs ("Sit-n-spins" or "dizzy discs")
-Collage materials (yarn, fabric, and confetti, items from nature, shape cut-outs, cotton, buttons, and magazine pictures) and small cardboard boxes, Styrofoam trays, paper tubes, etc.
-Crafting materials (stencils, stickers, stamps/ washable ink pads)
-Musical instruments (bells, shakers, drums, cymbals, keyboards, musical tapes)
- Tactile toys (koosh balls, crush balls, squeeze toys, bean bags, beanie babies)

Sunday Class Schedule

Date_____

Lesson_____

9:00   Student Check In

- Parents/Guardians Check in Students
- Parents/Teachers take note of "Teacher/Student Partnerships" and help student transition into the classroom

9:00-9:25   Learning Center Time
              (Assisting teachers work one on one with students at centers)

- The "Cozy Corner" with Books & Audio-Visual_____
- Gross Motor or Action Center_____
- Sensory or "Hands on" Center_____
- Fine Motor/Visual Center _____
- Art Center_____
- Writing/Game Center_____
- Music Center_____

9:25-9:30   Clean Up Time/Bathroom Break
              (Assisting teachers/students clean up centers)

9:30-9:40   Bible Time
              (Assisting teachers will guide students to Bible time and remain seated with them)

- Story/Prayer
- Songs
- Creative Movement

9:40-9:55   Craft
              (Assisting teachers help individual students with craft and clean up)

9:55-10:00   Closing Activity and/or Singing
              Prayer
              (Assisting teachers will guide students to closing time and remain seated with them)

10:00   Student Check Out

- Students are released to parents/guardians only
- Teachers/parents communicate briefly about the student's progress

Permission to photocopy this handout granted for local church use.
© 2007 Amy Rapada

Following the Sunday Class Schedule

❖ Set-Up/Preparation

The set up and preparation of the Special Needs class is extremely important and the key to providing students with a successful learning experience. Hours are spent each week putting together new learning center activities, planning the Bible lesson and preparing the craft materials. For consistency, the structure of the classroom arrangement is kept the same each week. Although these tasks are time consuming, the rewards are great. I hope that you will see that today and that you will be inspired by and touched by the work that God can do through you in the special needs ministry.

Prayer

Next, before the students arrive, pray as a group and by name for them. Join hands with all the volunteers and ask God to help each student be a successful learner. He will answer your prayers.

❖ Child Check In

- Each Sunday, special needs students and typical peers are welcomed into the Sunday school classroom.
- Parents or guardians check in their children by signing them in and writing any special instructions for the morning.
- Parents are then given pagers with silencers to take with them to Sunday service.
- As the students enter the classroom, parents and volunteers take note of the "teacher/student partnerships" board and help students to transition into the classroom.
- Occasionally, we have volunteers meet students at the car if requested by parents.

❖ Learning Center Time

Teaching in the special needs Sunday School class is based on a thematic approach to learning. We know that children learn by relating familiar concepts to new ideas. Therefore, each Sunday class offers a theme that is reinforced throughout the hour. Learning centers are used to introduce the day's theme. In addition to the thematic approach, we provide a sensory integration approach to learning. Because many kids with disabilities have trouble with sensory integration, our activities are designed to give them auditory, visual, kinesthetic and tactile input. During the "learning center" time, students work in small groups at student centered stations. Volunteers and peer tutors work to engage students in the center activities by modeling behaviors, using hand over hand guidance when needed, giving simple prompts and cues and allowing students to be as independent as possible.

Use learning centers to introduce the Biblical concepts. If the lesson is "Jesus Blesses the Children" design activities that incorporate that concept. For example at the gross motor center, students might be asked to jump on the trampoline while practicing a correlating Bible verse. At the writing center, they may write short stories (with the help of a volunteer if needed) on how Jesus has blessed them. The fine motor center could entail doing puzzles of children. Activities with varying degrees of difficulty should be presented.

❖ Clean Up Time

Transitioning is difficult for many children. Because of this, "clean up time" in the special needs classroom is made to be fun and non-threatening. A visual signal and song is used to carefully guide students to circle time to listen to the Bible lesson.

Opening

Begin lessons with a familiar routine or opening such as: "Who's come to Sunday school today, if it's you say your name when I point your way," and "The Bible says that Jesus was loving, kind and good. I want to live as Jesus did and do the things I should," and "The B-I-B-L-E, yes that's the book for me, I stand alone on the word of God, the B-I-B-L-E." The age of your students will determine your selections of songs and poems.

❖ Bible Time

Assisting teachers guide students to Bible time and remain seated with them. Students are greeted individually and then, as a group, join in a Bible song and poem. A new Bible story is read each Sunday. Stories that have colorful visuals and predictable patterns help to maintain the attention of the kids. Children are asked to actively participate in the story, each at his or her own level. Reading sentences aloud, using sign language, gesturing and acting with props are some of the ways that students stay engaged in the lesson.

❖ Craft Time

To reinforce the lesson, assisting teachers help students with a hands-on art activity. A wide variety of craft materials is provided to meet the sensory needs of students. The projects encourage creativity and self expression.

❖ Singing Time

Provide music or singing time. Children with disabilities especially love music!! I have seen wonderful responses from children during this time. Music is therapeutic. You probably already know who some of the musicians are in your church. Find out if one or two of them can be available to come in weekly and play songs for these children. What a gift they will be giving!!

Each Sunday session concludes with songs about Jesus. The hope is that as the children leave each Sunday, they'll carry Jesus with them all week long. As their spirits are uplifted, so too will be those of others who have taken part in the special needs ministry.

Learning Center Set Up:

Learning centers are well-defined workspaces for students to learn using hands on materials. Centers should be set up in an organized manner. Signs should be placed throughout the special needs classroom to designate areas (See curriculum center descriptions, pages 57-137). Each center can be clearly labeled with directions to provide both students and volunteers with instructions for activities.

Center Supplies Needed:

1. Book Corner a comfy space, large cushions, pillows or mats, a blanket or two, various levels/genre of Christian books, a large book basket or container, a tape player and books on tape

2. Sensory Center a sensory table or tub filled with a good supply of a tactile substance (Examples: sand, rice, bubbles, water, cotton balls, straw, ice-cubes, corn meal, flour, leaves, soil and seeds, confetti, shaving cream, lentils or dried beans, pebbles, playdough, clay)

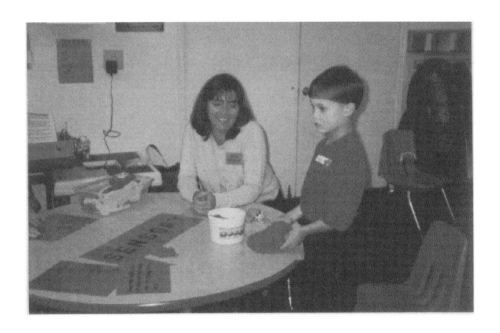

3. Fine Motor Center puzzles, manipulatives such as building blocks, legos, cubes, peg boards, wooden beads, lacing cards, tinker toys, sorting toys and other small motor activities

4. Art Center a wide variety of craft supplies such as paper, paints, crayons, markers, glue and collage materials (yarn, fabric, confetti, glitter, items from nature, shape cut-outs, cotton, buttons, magazine pictures) and cardboard boxes, styrofoam trays, paper tubes, etc.

5. Music Center a piano if available, musical instruments such as bells, shakers, drums, cymbals, etc. and song books, musical tapes and a tape player

6. Writing Center different types of writing materials such as pencils, pens, markers, crayons, paint, chalk, alphabet/picture stamps, ink pads, stencils, alphabet/picture sponge cutouts

7. Game Center an assortment of board and card and electronic games at various age levels

8. Gross Motor Center a tumbling mat, mini trampoline, therapy balls, sensory discs, scooter, hoola hoops, jump rope, squeeze toys and other large muscle activities

➡Conceptual Lessons for Students with Special Needs

Special Needs Learning Center Set Up
Concept- Faithfulness (week 1)

Preschool/ Primary and Intermediate/ Middle School:

Supplies- mini trampolines, play tunnel, therapy ball spinning discs, scooter

---

***Gross Motor Center**- March on the mini trampoline. Say this verse as you march: "By faith the walls of Jericho fell down." Hebrews 11:30

Supplies- legos, wooden blocks, waffle blocks, foam blocks, cube blocks and other building manipulatives

---

***Fine Motor Center**- Build the walls of Jericho. Make your walls big and tall. Now watch the walls come tumbling down. God helped the Israelites because they obeyed Him.

Supplies-various sized boxes, cans, containers, paper rolls, glue, crayons, markers, scissors, colored construction paper

---

***Art Center**- Build the city of Jericho. Be as creative as you can. God asked the Israelites to march around this city seven times for seven days. Joshua thought this was strange but he loved and obeyed God, anyways. God will do great things for those who are faithful to Him.

Supplies-children's Bibles and books set out on story mat with cushions

---

***Cuddly Corner/Cozy Corner Center**- Read the story of "The Fall of Jericho," Joshua 5:1, 10-15; 6

Supplies-sensory table and/ or individual tubs filled with sand, people figures

----

*Sensory Center- Set the people of the "Lord's Army" in the dry ground. Now they are ready to fight the battle of Jericho. Think about a time that you fought a battle for God. What have you done to be faithful and strong?

Special Needs Learning Center Set Up
Concept- Forgiveness (week 2)

Preschool/ Primary and Intermediate/ Middle School:

Supplies- mini trampolines, play tunnel, spinning disc, scooter, therapy balls

----

*Gross Motor Center- Practice this Bible verse while moving on the big equipment: "If you forgive, your heavenly Father will forgive you." Matthew 6:14

Supplies-legos, Lincoln logs, wooden blocks, tinker toys, stained glass builders, cubes, and other building manipulatives

----

*Fine Motor Center- Build the house of Paul in Rome. Paul welcomed the runaway slave into his home. He taught him about forgiveness. He helped him to ask for forgiveness.

Supplies-colored construction paper, people cut outs, glue sticks, markers, crayons, fabric pieces, yarn pieces

----

*Art Center- To be forgiven makes us feel whole again. Put together the pieces to make a whole person. Have an adult help you to write FORGIVENESS on your paper.

Supplies-Children's Bibles and books set out on a story mat with cushions

----
*Cuddly Corner/Cozy Corner Center-Read the story of "A Runaway Slave" in The Book of Philemon.

Supplies-sensory table and/ or individual tubs filled with bubble containers and blowers

----
*Sensory Center-We must forgive if we want to be forgiven. Blow bubbles. After you blow, say: "I forgive _____ for _____." Continue blowing bubbles. ☺

❖ ❖ ❖ ❖ ❖ ❖ ❖ ❖ ❖ ❖ ❖ ❖ ❖

Special Needs Learning Center Set Up
Concept- Holiness (week 3)

<u>Preschool/ Primary and Intermediate/ Middle School:</u>

Supplies- trampoline, therapy ball, disc, scooter, play tunnel

----
*Gross Motor Center- Pretend to travel across the desert as the Wise Men did in Search of the Christ child. Say this Bible verse, while you crawl, bounce, jump, or scoot: "Ye shall...find me when ye shall search for me with all your heart." Jeremiah 29:13

Supplies- pattern blocks, legos, wooden and plastic tinker toys, stained glass toys, Christmas puzzles

----
*Fine Motor Center- Build the star that led the Wise Men to Jesus. God asks us to desire and know Jesus. He asks us to show holiness to Him.

Supplies- **Preschool/Primary**: *star ornament cut outs, red yarn ties, red/ green/gold macaroni, glue, crayons, hole punchers-* **Intermediate/Middle School:** *wise men cut outs, black or dark blue construction paper, star cut outs, star confetti, glue, markers, crayons*

----

*Art Center- Preschool/Primary: Make a star ornament for your tree. The Wise Men followed the star that led to Baby Jesus...the new holy King.

---

*Art Center –Intermediate/Middle School: Make a picture of the Wise Men. Add the stars in the sky. Be sure to add the brightest star that the Wise Men followed to see Baby Jesus...the new holy King.

Supplies- *Children's Bibles and books, Matthew 2; set on mat with cushions*

----

*Cuddly Corner/Cozy Corner Center- Read the story of "A Star Leads the Wise Men to Jesus, Matthew 2

Supplies- *sensory table or individual sensory tubs filled with straw, Nativity figures and animals*

----

*Sensory Center- Create your own Nativity scene in the straw, especially adding the Wise Men and the gifts that they brought to Jesus.

❖ ❖ ❖ ❖ ❖ ❖ ❖ ❖ ❖ ❖ ❖ ❖ ❖

Special Needs Learning Center Set Up
Concept-Protection (week 4)

Preschool/ Primary and Intermediate/ Middle School:

Supplies- mini trampolines, play tunnels, therapy balls, spinning discs, scooter

----

*Gross Motor Center- Practice this Bible verse: "The Lord preserves and protects all them that love Him." Psalms 145:20 Say this verse as you move on the big equipment.

Supplies-legos, wooden blocks, tinker toys, waffle blocks, stained glass builders, cubes and other building manipulatives

----

*Fine Motor Center- Build tall giants. The Israelites were afraid of the Giants, but God wanted them to trust in Him. When we think of all that God has done for us in the past, we will not be afraid of the future. We know that God will protect us.

Supplies –Preschool/Primary: people cut outs, construction paper, glue, large crayons; Intermediate/ Middle School: cut out clocks, clock hands, picture activities, glue, scissors, and small crayons

----

*Art Center- Preschool/Primary: We will not be afraid if we remember that God is with us and will protect us. Put together a person that looks like you. Say: God is always with me. God protects me. Intermediate/ Middle School: We will not be afraid if we remember that God is with us always. As you put together your clock, add pictures that show the times that God is with you.

Supplies-Children's Bibles and books, story mat and cushions

----

*Cuddly Corner/Cozy Corner Center- Read the story "Afraid of Giants," Numbers 13:1-3, 17-33; 14

Supplies- sensory table and/or individual tubs filled with birdseed, people figures

----

*Sensory Center- Caleb and Joshua said, "With God on our side, we can defeat the Giants." Set Caleb and Joshua in the Promised Land of Canaan.

❖ ❖ ❖ ❖ ❖ ❖ ❖ ❖ ❖ ❖ ❖ ❖ ❖

Special Needs Learning Center Set Up
Concept- Courage (week 5)

<u>Preschool/ Primary and Intermediate/ Middle School:</u>

Supplies-trampoline, therapy ball, play tunnel, spinning disc, scooter, hula hoop

----

*Gross Motor Center- Try a new physical activity that is difficult for you. Ask God to help you with your activity while you practice this Bible verse: "The Lord said unto him, surely I will be with thee." Judges 6:16

Supplies- wooden blocks, legos, stained glass window blocks, waffle blocks, tinker toys, Lincoln logs and other building blocks

----

*Fine Motor Center- Build the homes of Israel. God chose Gideon to save the city of Israel from the Midianites, who were warriors. This was difficult for Gideon. When God asks us to do something difficult, he will help us to do it. He will give us the courage that we need.

Supplies- Gideon figure cut outs, wheat/ straw, angel figure cut outs, bits of gold ribbons and fabric, glue, markers, crayons, construction paper

----

*Art Center- One day when Gideon was working in the wheat fields, an angel appeared to him. The angel had been sent by God and delivered this message to Gideon: "God is with you." God is with YOU also. Make a picture of Gideon or the angel. Add wheat to the field with Gideon. Add gold sparkles to the angel.

Supplies- Children's Bibles and storybooks set out on mat with cushions. (Soft people puppets can be added to act out the story).

----

*Cuddly Corner/Cozy Corner Center- Read the story of "An Angel Appears to Gideon" in Judges 6.

Supplies- sensory table or individual sensory tubs filled with rice, plastic army figures

----

*Sensory Center- God told Gideon to assemble an army to help save the people of Israel. He asked him to lead the army against the Midianites. We can also ask God to lead in our lives as He did in Gideon's life. We can ask God to give us courage. Assemble your own army by setting up the plastic figures in the rice.

Special Needs Learning Center Set Up
Concept- Love (week 6)

Preschool/ Primary and Intermediate/ Middle School:

Supplies- trampoline, therapy ball, play tunnel, spinning disc, scooter

----

*Gross Motor Center- As you move on the big equipment pretend to travel to Bethlehem. Practice saying this Bible verse: "Thou shall call His name Jesus for He shall save His people from their sins."

Supplies- an assortment of blocks (wooden blocks, Lincoln logs, legos, pattern blocks. etc.), baby Jesus, Mary, and Joseph figures.

----

*Fine Motor Center- Build the manger that baby Jesus was placed in as a cradle. Create the stable where Jesus was born. Add Mary and Joseph to your stable. Can you feel the love that Jesus brought into the world?

Supplies-preschool/primary- large manger and baby Jesus cut outs, brown construction paper, glue sticks, hay, and felt squares; intermediate/ middle school: stable cut out with small Mary, Joseph, baby Jesus and animal cut outs, brown construction paper, glue sticks, wooden craft sticks, hay

---

*Art Center- preschool/ primary- Make the manger where baby Jesus was born in Bethlehem. Put swaddling clothes on Jesus and place hay in the manger. Now lay baby Jesus in the manger just as Mary did. Jesus is our Savior born in Bethlehem, sent to us in love.

---

*Art Center-intermediate/ middle school**:** Glue the stable, Mary, Joseph, baby Jesus and animals to your paper. God promised that out of love a Savior would be born in Bethlehem to a woman named Mary. Who was the Savior?

Supplies- Children's Bibles and Christmas stories set out on mat with cushions

---

*Cuddly Corner/Cozy Corner Center- Read the story of "Baby Jesus is born," Luke 2:1-7.

Supplies- sensory table or individual tubs filled with hay/ straw, farm animal figures and small boxes or strawberry baskets

---

*Sensory Center- In the midst of cows, horses, and donkeys, the Son of God was born. Put warm hay in the mangers. Place the animals close by to welcome baby Jesus. What love there was that day!

❖ ❖ ❖ ❖ ❖ ❖ ❖ ❖ ❖ ❖ ❖ ❖ ❖

Special Needs Learning Center Set Up
Concept-Patience (week 7)

Preschool/ Primary and Intermediate/ Middle School:

Supplies-mini trampolines play tunnels, scooter, spinning discs, therapy ball

----

*Gross Motor Center- Jump, crawl, scoot, spin, or bounce softly. Practice this Bible verse while on the big equipment: "A soft answer turns away wrath." Proverbs 15:1

Supplies- puzzles of people (wooden framed puzzles, jigsaws, linking people, people stringing beads, etc.)

----

*Fine Motor Center- Put together the puzzles of people. Nabal was Abigail's husband and he was not kind to David and others. Abigail did her best to be patient with others. God showed her that it pays to be patient and kind.

Supplies- preschool/primary: large heart cutouts, magazine cut outs, small heart cutouts, people cut outs, glue, crayons; intermediate/ middle school: heart cut outs, people cut outs, beads, string, markers, glue

----

*Art Center- preschool/ primary: Make a "Be Patient' heart collage. Glue pictures of people being patient to one another onto your heart. God teaches us to be kind and patient to others.

----

*Art Center- intermediate/ middle school: Make a "kindness" necklace. String beads onto your Jesus heart. God teaches us to be kind and patient with others.

Supplies- Children's Bibles and books set on story mat with cushions

---

*Cuddly Corner/Cozy Corner Center- Read the story about "Brave Beautiful Abigail." 1 Samuel 25

Supplies- bright, colorful fish rocks, containers, cups, utensils (Note: Be sure to know the sensory needs of students before trying this particular center as some kids think these rocks look like candy and might try to mouth them.)

---

*Sensory Center- Abigail was always kind and patient with others. God blessed her because of this. As you work with the bright and colorful rocks, think of ways that you can be kind and patient with others to brighten their days.

Special Needs Learning Center Set Up
Concept- Witnessing (week 8)

Preschool/ Primary and Intermediate/ Middle School:

Supplies- mat, trampoline, scooter, play tunnel, discs

---

*Gross Motor Center- Practice this verse while bouncing, scooting, or crawling to Syria. "Train up a child in the way he should go." Proverbs 22:6

Supplies- peg boards, tinker toys, cubes, other counting toys

---

*Fine Motor Center- King Naaman was told, "Go and bathe in the River Jordan seven times and you will be cured." Use peg boards, tinker toys, cubes, and other counting toys to count to 7. Make many groups of 7 and total your groups.

Supplies- crown outlines, crown cut outs from fabric and felt, scrolls made from paper rolls glued to Popsicle sticks, people cut-outs, drinking straws cut into 1 inch pieces, plastic string or cord

----

*Art Center- (preschool/ primary) Make King Naamans crown. God taught him that a child can witness for Jesus.

---

 *Art Center- (intermediate/ middle school) Elisha the prophet sent King Naaman a message about the one true God. Write a message on a scroll to tell a friend or witness about Jesus, or make a "messenger necklace" to wear when you share about God.

Supplies-Children's books and Bibles set out on story mat with cushions

----

*Cuddly Corner/Cozy Corner Center- Read stories in the Bible about "The Captive Maid." 2 Kings 5

Supplies-sensory table or individual tubs filled with sand and toy people figures

----

*Sensory Center- A young girl wanted her master to see the prophet Elisha. Elisha told the master, Naaman to travel to his house to be cured by God. Naaman traveled through the sand to get to Elisha's house. Make a path in the sand and add people to your path. These are people that you can witness to.

❖ ❖ ❖ ❖ ❖ ❖ ❖ ❖ ❖ ❖ ❖ ❖ ❖

Special Needs Learning Center Set Up
Concept-Trust (week 9)

Preschool/ Primary and Intermediate/ Middle School:

Supplies- mini trampolines, therapy balls, play tunnel, scooter, spinning discs

---

*Gross Motor Center- Say this Bible verse while jumping "tall" on the big equipment. "You come to me with a sword; I come in the name of the Lord." 1 Samuel 17

Supplies-An assortment of blocks and building manipulatives (legos, unifix cubes, circle stackers, waffle blocks, etc.

---

*Fine Motor Center- Build tall giants like Goliath. God will help us when we have "giant" problems, just as he helped David.

Supplies- Preschool: large stones, paint brushes, water containers, mixed tempera paint in various colors, Intermediate/ Middle School: fabric strips, hole punchers, cord, wooden bottle tops, glue

---

*Art Center- preschool- Paint the stones that David used to defeat the Giant. David trusted in God to help him

---

*Art Center- intermediate/ middle school- Make the sling shot that David used to defeat the Giant. Put five smooth stones on your sling shot. David trusted in God to help him.

Supplies-Children's Bibles and stories of "David and Goliath," cushions, story mat

---

*Cuddly Corner/Cozy Corner Center- Read the story of "David and Goliath." 1Samuel 17

Supplies- sensory table and individual tubs filled with bird seed and containers/ scoops

---

*Sensory Center- God will do great things for us if we trust Him. As you work in the bird seed, talk about how you can trust God in your life.

❖ ❖ ❖ ❖ ❖ ❖ ❖ ❖ ❖ ❖ ❖ ❖ ❖

Special Needs Learning Center Set Up
Concept- Believing (week 10)

Preschool/ Primary and Intermediate/ Middle School:

Supplies- mini trampoline, therapy ball, scooter, disc, play tunnel, hula hoop

----

*Gross Motor Center- Jump on the trampoline. Bounce on the big ball, scoot on the scooter, etc. with your eyes closed. (Have a volunteer help you with this.) Practice this Bible verse: "Blessed are they that have not seen yet have believed." John 20:29

Supplies- "I Spy" puzzles and games, treasure boxes and bags filled with small toys, magnifying glasses, sunglasses, and flashlights

----

*Fine Motor Center- "Those who seek will find." Seek to find the toys and objects using magnifying glasses, sunglasses and flashlights. Did you believe first without seeing?

Supplies- sunglass patterns, glue, tape, scissors, heart patterns, heart cards, felt heart cut outs, sticker eyes

----

*Art Center- Jesus wants us to **see (and believe) with our hearts.** Make a pair of seeing glasses. Decorate hearts with heart cutouts and sticker eyes.

Supplies- Children's Bibles and storybooks set out on cushions with pillows

----

*Cuddly Corner/Cozy Corner Center- Read the stories about "Doubting Thomas." John 20:24-31

Supplies- sensory table or individual tubs filled with sand, toy people figures, cups and containers

----

*Sensory Center- We don't need to doubt that Jesus is alive today. We have proof and can believe from the words of the Bible and from other Christians. Talk about what proof you have that Jesus is alive in your life.   Build a church with sand and put the people inside.

❖ ❖ ❖ ❖ ❖ ❖ ❖ ❖ ❖ ❖ ❖ ❖ ❖

Special Needs Learning Center Set Up
Concept- Helping (week 11)

Preschool/ Primary and Intermediate/ Middle School:

Supplies- trampoline, therapy ball, tumbling mat, play tunnel, scooter, hula hoop, spinning disc

----

*Gross Motor Center- Help a friend to learn a new skill on the big equipment. Practice this verse together: "With God all things are possible." Matthew 19:26

Supplies- building blocks, cubes, legos, Lincoln logs, kinex, tinker toys, waffle blocks, and other building manipulatives

----

 *Fine Motor Center- Build the building that Elisha and his prophets built next to the Jordan River. God helped them with their building. When the ax that they were using became lost in the water, Elisha made it appear.

Supplies- preschool/ primary: paper plates, vegetable cut outs, crayons, glue, dried beans; intermediate/ middle school: paper sacks, barley bread cut outs, corn ear cut outs, oats, popcorn kernels, markers, glue
----
*Art Center- preschool/ primary: Make the stew that Elisha asked his prophets to make. Glue vegetable seeds and cut outs to your plate. Elisha asked God to purify the food. God made it safe for the people to eat.

----

*Art Center- intermediate/ middle school: Make the loaves of barley bread and ears of corn by gluing oats onto bread slices and popped popcorn kernels onto the corn. Put your food in a sack, as the prophets did. Elisha told 100 people that "The Lord said there would be plenty for all." The Lord helped and there was.

Supplies- Children's Bibles and storybooks on mat with cushions
----
*Cuddly Corner/Cozy Corner Center- Read the story of "Elisha, Prophet of God," 2 Kings 4:38-44; 6:1-7

Supplies- sensory table or individual tubs filled with cornmeal, cups, plates, bowls, mixing spoons
----
*Sensory Center- Cook a meal for your family. Ask God to bless your meal. God likes to help us help others.

Special Needs Learning Center Set Up
Concept- Provision (week 12)

Preschool/ Primary and Intermediate/ Middle School:

Supplies- mini trampolines, therapy ball, play tunnel, scooter, spinning disc

----

*Gross Motor Center- Practice this Bible verse with a friend on the big equipment: "Let us not love in word, but in deed and truth." 1 John 3:18

Supplies- legos, Lincoln logs, cubes, wooden blocks, waffle blocks, stained glass builders, and other building manipulatives, small children's pots and pans

----

*Fine Motor Center- Build the widow's house. Put pots and pans inside of her home. God's prophet Elisha told her to fill her pots with oil. God provided enough oil to fill all of her pots! God will provide for us also.

Supplies- Preschool/Primary-happy and sad face cut outs, paper lunch sacks, eye stickers, yarn for hair, glue, crayons; Intermediate/Middle School- kindness card sheets, scissors, glue, construction paper, markers

----

*Art Center- preschool/primary- Make happy and sad puppets. When we love Jesus, we are kind to others; we can help them to feel happy. When we are not kind, this makes others feel sad.

---

*Art Center- Intermediate/Middle School- Cut out the kindness pictures and glue to construction paper to make a collage. Name the ways that we can be kind to others. God will provide for us when we are kind to others.

Supplies- children's Bibles and books placed on story mat with cushions

----

*Cuddly Corner/Cozy Corner Center- Read the story of "Elisha Helps a Widow." 2 Kings 4:1-7

Supplies- sensory table and/ or individual tubs filled with colorful fish rocks, coins sprinkled in rocks

----

*Sensory Center- Look for the coins hidden in the rocks. God surprised the widow by giving her the money that she needed. God will surprise us with His provisions when we are kind to others.

Special Needs Learning Center Set Up
Concept-Grace (week 13)

Preschool/ Primary and Intermediate/ Middle School:

Supplies-mini trampolines play tunnel, scooter, spinning discs, therapy balls

----

*Gross Motor Center- Practice this verse while thinking of a time when someone was unkind to you. "Forgive and you will be forgiven." Luke 6:37

Supplies-pegs and peg boards, stringing beads, cubes, counting blocks, number puzzles, number flash cards

----

*Fine Motor Center- Jesus told Peter that he should forgive seven times seventy seven times. Jesus meant that we should forgive again and again. Practice your counting and then say: "Through God's Grace, I will forgive again and again."

Supplies-poster paper, paint brushes, an assortment of mixed tempera paints, handy-wipes, painting smocks or aprons

----

*Art Center- Forgiving others is the way to greatest happiness. God's Grace makes it possible for us to forgive others. Paint a giant happy face or many happy faces. Make your painting bright and colorful!!

Supplies-Children's Bibles and storybooks, story mat with cushions, people puppets

----

*Cuddly Corner/Cozy Corner Center- Read the story of "Forgiving One Another," Matthew 18:21-25. Now act out the story with the people puppets.

Supplies-sensory table and/or individual tubs filled with bubbles, bubble blowers

----

*Sensory Center- As you blow bubbles, watch them go into the air. When we ask God to help us forgive someone, we let go of our feelings of anger and hurt, just as we let go of bubbles blowing….

Supplies- sensory table and/ or individual tubs filled with colorful fish rocks, coins sprinkled in rocks

----

*Sensory Center- Look for the coins hidden in the rocks. God surprised the widow by giving her the money that she needed. God will surprise us with His provisions when we are kind to others.

❖   ❖   ❖   ❖   ❖   ❖   ❖   ❖   ❖   ❖   ❖   ❖   ❖

Special Needs Learning Center Set Up
Concept-Obedience (week 14)

Preschool/ Primary and Intermediate/ Middle School:

Supplies-mini trampolines play tunnel, scooter, spinning discs, therapy balls, tumbling mats

----

*Gross Motor Center- Hold onto a friend's hand while you move on the big equipment. Now say this Bible verse together: "And the Lord shall guide thee continually." Isaiah 58:11

Supplies-small legos, duplos, Lincoln logs, stained glass builders, wooden blocks, pegs and boards, cubes, plastic tinker toys

----

*Fine Motor Center- Abram (later named Abraham) built an altar to worship God. He wanted to talk to God often so that he would remember to do what is right and obedient. Now, you build an altar to God. Pray that God will help you to do what is right and obedient.

Supplies-Abraham and Lot face cut-outs, animal cut-outs, paper lunch sacks, glue sticks, crayons, markers, fabric squares, cotton balls, scissors

----

*Art Center- Abram was very kind to his nephew Lot. He let him choose first the land for his animals and said that he would take what was left. God had helped Abram to not be selfish. Make some paper bag puppets of Abraham, Lot and animals. Act out Abram's unselfishness. Abram was obedient to God.

Supplies-Children's books and Bibles set out on story mat with cushions, stuffed animals

----

*Cuddly Corner/Cozy Corner Center- Read the story of "God Blesses Faithful Abraham," Genesis 11:27-32; 12; 13.

Supplies-sensory table and/or individual tubs filled with soil, gardening tools or scoops, seeds, planting cups

----

*Sensory Center- God said to Abram "go to a land that I will show you." Abram trusted and obeyed God. He learned to love his new land. Plant some new land in a garden container. Ask God to help you trust and obey Him in all that you do."

❖ ❖ ❖ ❖ ❖ ❖ ❖ ❖ ❖ ❖ ❖ ❖ ❖

Special Needs Learning Center Set Up
Concept- Reverence (week 15)

Preschool/ Primary and Intermediate/ Middle School:

Supplies-mini trampolines, therapy balls, play tunnel, scooter, spinning discs

----

*Gross Motor Center- Practice this Bible verse while moving on the big equipment: "The place where thou stands is holy ground."

Supplies-Lincoln logs, wooden blocks, stained glass builders, cubes, legos and other building manipulatives

----

*Fine Motor Center- We can do any task, large or small, when God calls us. With His help, we can succeed. Build the Egyptian palace where Pharaoh lived. God told Moses that Pharaoh would see Hs great power and let the people leave Egypt. Moses trusted God and had reverence or respect for Him.

Supplies-lacing shoe pattern cut outs, plastic cord, markers, crayons, stickers

----

*Art Center- God told Moses to take off his shoes, because he was standing on holy ground. Moses was chosen by God to lead the people out of Egypt. Make a pair of shoes for yourself. Let these be your "holy ground" shoes and lead others to be reverent to God.

Supplies-Children's books and Bibles set out on story mat with cushions

----

*Cuddly Corner/Cozy Corner Center- Read the story of "God Speaks to Moses." Exodus 2:11-25; 3

Supplies-sensory table or individual tubs filled with rice, cups and containers

----

*Sensory Center- We should show reverence to God. As you play with the rice, think of ways to be respectful to God.

❖ ❖ ❖ ❖ ❖ ❖ ❖ ❖ ❖ ❖ ❖ ❖ ❖

Special Needs Learning Center Set Up
Concept-Prayer (week 16)

Preschool/ Primary and Intermediate/ Middle School:

Supplies-mini trampolines, scooter, therapy ball, spinning discs, play tunnel

----

*Gross Motor Center- Practice this memory verse as you have a safe time on the big equipment: "Whoever trusts in the Lord shall be safe." Proverbs 29:25

Supplies-puzzles with people, linking people, tinker toys, legos with people attachments, stringing wooden people shaped beads, picture cards/ worksheets, scissors

----

*Fine Motor Center- Put together the people puzzles and activities. Use scissors to cut on the dotted lines of the picture cards. Practice naming the times that God hears our prayers. "God hears my prayers when I am with my family; God hears my prayers at night, God hears my prayers when I am scared…"

Supplies-play dough of various colors, people and heart cookie cutter shapes, rolling pins, an assortment of tools/ utensils

----

*Art Center- Create people, praying hands, and God's loving heart shapes. God hears our prayers and He always does what is best for us.

Supplies-Children's Bibles and stories set out on story mat with cushions, people puppets

----

*Cuddly Corner/Cozy Corner Center- Read the story of "Hezekiah Trusts God," 2 Kings 18:1-18, 17; 19:1-19, 20:1-11, 35-36

Supplies-sensory table and/or individual tubs filled with soil, gardening tools and seeds

----

*Sensory Center- Plant a small garden for God. He hears our prayers and helps us to "grow in faith." Care for your plant as God cares for you. God keeps us safe. Say a prayer of thanks to God.

<u>Special Needs Learning Center Set Up</u>
<u>Concept-Healing (week 17)</u>

<u>Preschool/ Primary and Intermediate/ Middle School:</u>

Supplies- mini trampoline, therapy ball, scooter, disc, play tunnel

----

*Gross Motor Center- Practice this verse while jumping, bouncing or spinning. "Be not afraid, only believe." Mark 5:36

Supplies- wooden blocks, soft blocks, Lincoln logs, stained glass blocks, waffle blocks, legos

----

*Fine Motor Center- If we trust Jesus, He will do what is best for us. When Jesus went to the house of Jairus, He said, "Don't be afraid, just trust Me." Then He made Jairus's daughter well again. Build the house of Jairus. As you build, think about how you can trust Jesus to heal more in your life.

Supplies- door hangars/ cards: get well door hangar patterns, folded construction paper cards large, crayons, stickers, decorative foam pieces, glue; houses: house patterns, glue, stickers, small crayons, people cut outs

---

*Art Center- preschool/primary- Jesus can do miracles if we ask Him to. Make "Get Well" door hangars and cards to give to someone who is sick. Ask God to heal and make this person feel better.

---

*Art Center-intermediate/ middle school- The age of miracles has not passed. Jesus can do all that we ask if only we believe in Him. Create the house where Jesus healed Jairus. Share your house with someone and tell them about the miracle of Jesus

---

Supplies- Children's Bibles and storybooks set out on mat with cushions and blanket

---

*Cuddly Corner/Cozy Corner Center- Read the Bible stories about how "Jesus Raised Jairus's Daughter." Mark 5:21-43 (Kids can also lie down and pretend to be Jairus's daughter, who when she is miraculously healed, stands up and walks)

Supplies- sensory table or individual tubs filled with sand, toy people figures

---

*Sensory Center- Jesus and His friends stepped ashore. A crowd of people were there to welcome Him. One man fell to his feet and asked Jesus to come heal his daughter. Place the crowd of people in the sand. Say a prayer to Jesus and ask Him to heal someone who is sick.

❖ ❖ ❖ ❖ ❖ ❖ ❖ ❖ ❖ ❖ ❖ ❖ ❖

<u>Special Needs Learning Center Set Up</u>
<u>Concept-Rejoicing (week 18)</u>

<u>Preschool/ Primary and Intermediate/ Middle School:</u>

Supplies- mini trampolines, play tunnels, spinning discs, scooter, therapy balls

---

*Gross Motor Center- Practice this Bible verse while on the big equipment with your hand on your heart: "Trust in the Lord with all your heart; and lean not on your own understanding." Proverbs 3:5

Supplies-preschool/ primary- Jesus cut-outs, cross cut-outs, foam heart pieces, glue sticks, dot markers, large crayons, ; intermediate/ middle school: bread and drink cut-outs, cross cut outs, paper plates, dot markers, small crayons, glue sticks, bread crumbs

---

*Art Center-preschool/ primary- Make a loving Jesus cross to show that you will trust in Jesus with all of your heart. Add hearts to your cross. Rejoice because Jesus is alive!

---

*Art Center-intermediate/ middle school- Make a special plate for Jesus. Put bread, drink, and a cross on your plate. Add bread crumbs to your plate. The disciples did not recognize Jesus until they saw Him break bread for them. Then they began to worship Him. With great joy they said, "Jesus is alive."

Supplies-Children's Easter stories and Bibles set out on story mat; springtime stuffed animals may be added

---

*Cuddly Corner/Cozy Corner Center- Read the story "Jesus Appears to His Disciples." Luke 24:13-40; John 20:19-21

Supplies-sensory table and/ or individual sensory tubs filled with cotton balls, small Easter baskets

---

*Sensory Center- Jesus died for our sins. We can rejoice in the wonderful news that He did this for us before He rose into the heavens. Put heavenly cotton balls in your Easter baskets and say, "Jesus died for me."

Supplies- recorders, keyboards, musical toys, egg shakers, bells, maracas and other musical instruments

----

*Music Center- When Jesus appeared to His disciples they were amazed and excited. They went to spread the news that Jesus was alive! Let us rejoice in this also as we play our musical instruments.

Special Needs Learning Center Set Up
Concept-Righteousness (week 19)

Preschool/ Primary and Intermediate/ Middle School:

Supplies-mini trampolines, therapy balls, play tunnels, scooter, and spinning discs

----

*Gross Motor Center- Practice this Bible verse while playing on the big equipment: "Watch and pray, that ye enter not into temptation." Matthew 26: 41

Supplies- spring puzzles (animals, nature, and people outdoors), colorful building toys and blocks

----

*Fine Motor Center- As you work, say a quiet prayer to God. Ask Him to help you to do what is right or righteous.

Supplies-cupcake holders, coffee filters, pipe cleaners, beads, dot markers, tissue paper, scissors, tape

----

*Art Center- Create the flowers of the Gethsemane Garden. After Jesus prayed in this Garden, He was crucified for us, because He loves us!!

Supplies- Children's Bibles and storybooks set out on story mat

----

*Cuddly Corner/Cozy Corner Center- Read the story of "Jesus' Prayer for Help," Matthew 26:35-56; John 18:1-14. Now… you say a prayer for help to be righteous as Jesus is.

Supplies- sensory table and/ or individual tubs filled with dried lentils, gardening tools, cups and various shaped containers

----

*Sensory Center- Jesus prayed in the Garden of Gethsemane before he was crucified. Say a prayer to Jesus for righteousness, and then pretend to plant a small garden for Him.

<u>Special Needs Learning Center Set Up</u>
<u>Concept- Peace (week 20)</u>

<u>Preschool/ Primary and Intermediate/ Middle School:</u>

Supplies- mat, trampoline, therapy ball, play tunnel, sensory disc or scooter

----

*Gross Motor Center- Practice this Bible verse while moving like the wind and water on the trampoline, big ball, play tunnel, spinning disc or scooter. "He commanded the winds and water, and they obey Him." Luke 8:22-40

Supplies- assortment of wooden framed and jigsaw puzzles of children; simpler puzzles should be set out for younger class

----

*Fine Motor Center- "When we are afraid, we can trust Jesus." Do the puzzles of the children and discuss times when you have felt afraid and have trusted in Jesus. Did trusting in Him give you peace?

Supplies- boats: paper bowls, play dough, straws, triangle shaped pieces of paper towels, markers; textured pictures: stormy day picture outline, cotton balls, yellow paper 1" circle cut-outs, brown felt pieces, markers and glue

----

***Art Center**- preschool/ primary- Make a boat by filling a bowl with some play dough and placing a straw in the center of the dough. Use a triangle shaped piece of paper towel to attach to the straw for a sail. Jesus calmed the waters to teach us that we can trust in Him. We can be filled with His peace.

***Art Center-**intermediate/middle school- Create a textured picture of a stormy day. Use cotton for clouds, yellow paper cut outs for the sun and brown felt for land. Jesus will calm our stormy days and fill them with peace if we trust in Him.

Supplies- a variety of Children's Bibles and storybooks set out on a cushion with pillows

----

***Cuddly Corner/Cozy Corner Center**- Read Bible stories about how "Jesus Stills the Storm." Matthew 8:23-34. Mark 4:35 to 5:20

Supplies-sensory table or individual tubs filled with water and toy people figures, paper cups and a water pitcher filled with water

----

***Sensory Center**- Slowly add a cup of water to the water table that you are working at. Imagine being a disciple on the water that Jesus calmed. Say, "Peace, be still," just as Jesus did.

Special Needs Learning Center Set Up
Concept-Glorifying (week 21)

Preschool/ Primary and Intermediate/ Middle School:

Supplies-mini trampolines, scooter, therapy ball, play tunnels, spinning discs

---

*Gross Motor Center- As you move like the heavens and earth, say this Bible verse: "Thy will be done on earth, as it is in heaven." Matthew 6:10

Supplies- building blocks, legos, people figures, puzzles with people shapes, linking people

---

*Fine Motor Center- We are God's people and we can pray to Him and glorify His name. Build a church for the people and put together the people puzzles.

Supplies-foam bookmarks, lacing plastic cord, stickers

---

*Art Center- Jesus teaches us how to pray. He says: "Glory be to God." The Lord's Prayer is in our Bible. Make a bookmark to keep in your Bible to mark this place.

Supplies-children's books and Bibles set out on story mat or cushions

---

*Cuddly Corner/Cozy Corner Center- Read the Bible story of "Jesus Teaches Us How to Pray," Matthew 6:1-16; Luke 11:1-13

Supplies-sensory table and/or individual tubs filled with dried lima beans, scooping containers, planting cups

---

*Sensory Center- Pretend to plant seeds in God's earth. Say, "May Your will be done on earth, God." Now say: "For thine is the kingdom, the power and the glory to God."

Special Needs Learning Center Set Up
Concept- Repentance (week 22)

<u>Preschool/ Primary and Intermediate/ Middle School:</u>

Supplies-mini trampolines play tunnel, scooter, therapy balls, spinning discs

----

*Gross Motor Center- Practice this Bible verse with a forgiving friend: "If you forgive....your heavenly Father will also forgive you." Matthew 6:14

Supplies-a variety of Bible games such as Bible flash cards, Bible BINGO, sequence and pattern games, board games and hand held games

----

*Fine Motor Center- Play the games with one another. If a player makes a mistake, say "I forgive you for your mistake." Then encourage the other player to say: "I repent."

Supplies-dot markers, stamps, ink pads, crayons, bright shades of construction paper

----

*Art Center-Use the dot markers and stamps to create a happy and loving picture. Give your picture to someone who you need to ask forgiveness or repentance of.

Supplies-Children's Bibles and books set out on story mat with cushions

----

*Cuddly Corner/Cozy Corner Center-Read the story of "Joseph Forgives His Brothers," Genesis 44, 45.

Supplies-sensory table and/ or individual tubs filled with bubble mix, bubble blowers and wands

----

*Sensory Center- Blow bubbles up into the heavens and around your friends. Remember that God will forgive you as your forgive others and ask for repentance.

Special Needs Learning Center Set Up
Concept-Honor (week 23)

<u>Preschool/ Primary and Intermediate/ Middle School:</u>

Supplies- mini trampolines, play tunnels, scooter, spinning discs, therapy ball

----

*Gross Motor Center- Practice this Bible verse while jumping, bouncing or spinning: "For them that honor me, I will honor." 1 Samuel 2:30

Supplies- simple board games and puzzles

----

*Fine Motor Center- As you play a game or put together a puzzle with a friend, take special care to show kindness and honor to your friend. Now watch your friend show kindness and honor to you. Kindness and honor are repaid.

Supplies-heart and people shaped cookie cutters, rolling pins, cutting utensils, play dough or clay in various colors

----

 *Art Center- Ruth was a woman who showed much kindness and honor toward other people. Boaz was a man who showed much kindness and honor to others. Shape your dough into kindness hearts and honorable people cut outs. Jesus wants us to be kind and honorable to others.

Supplies- Children's books and Bible stories set out on story mat with cushions

----

*Cuddly Corner/Cozy Corner Center- Read the story of "Ruth and Boaz" in Ruth 2, 3, 4:13.

Supplies- sensory table or individual tubs filled with flour (whole wheat is less messy; provide aprons or smocks) cups and containers, dish filled with coins

----

*Sensory Center- Ruth and Naomi sold their grain and had money to buy food. Fill your containers with grain. Pretend to sell full containers to your neighbor. You may use the coins for buying. God will bless you for being kind and honorable to your neighbors.

Special Needs Learning Center Set Up
Concept-Sacrificing (week 24)

Preschool/ Primary and Intermediate/ Middle School:

Supplies-mini trampolines, therapy ball, scooter, spinning discs, play tunnels

----

*Gross Motor Center- Practice this Bible verse: "I, when lifted up from the earth, will draw all men to Me." John 12:32 Think about Jesus as you move on the big equipment and say this verse.

Supplies-wooden blocks, Lincoln logs, legos, tinker toys, stained glass builders, waffle blocks, cubes and other building manipulatives

----

*Fine Motor Center- Build the cross that Jesus died on. Jesus died to save us from our sins. He was crucified and sacrificed His life because He loved us so much.

Supplies-small cross cut outs, markers, glue, glitter, hole punchers, yarn, scissors

----

*Art Center- Make a cross necklace to wear. Let your necklace remind you that we should always do right for Jesus, who sacrificed His life for US.

Supplies-Children's books and Bibles set out on story mat with cushions

----

*Cuddly Corner/Cozy Corner Center- Read about "The Crucifixion," Matthew 27:1-54; Mark 15: 1-39; Luke 23:26-49; John 18:28-19:30.

Supplies-sensory table and or individual tubs filled with ice cubes

----

*Sensory Center-When Jesus died for us, He said, "if you believe in Me, you will be with Me in paradise." As you feel the cold ice cubes, think of ways that you can do right for Jesus by making your own sacrifices even when it is not popular to do so.

❖ ❖ ❖ ❖ ❖ ❖ ❖ ❖ ❖ ❖ ❖ ❖ ❖

<u>Special Needs Learning Center Set Up</u>
<u>Concept- Worshipping (week 25)</u>

<u>Preschool/ Primary and Intermediate/ Middle School:</u>

Supplies-mini trampolines, therapy balls, scooter, spinning discs, play tunnel

----

*Gross Motor Center- Practice this Bible verse, while thinking of God: "Thou shall have no other gods before me." Exodus 20:3

Supplies -a variety of jigsaw and wooden framed puzzles depicting people, linking people, duplos with people, people figures, stringing wooden "people" beads

----

*Fine Motor Center- As you put together people puzzles, remember that God is loving and forgiving of all people.

Supplies-an assortment of clay and molding utensils

----

*Art Center- The people made an idol out of gold and jewelry to worship. Moses destroyed the idol. Make an idol or false god out of clay. Now, destroy the idol. We should worship ONLY God.

Supplies-Children's books and Bibles set out on mats with cushions

----

*Cuddly Corner/Cozy Corner Center- Read the story of "The Golden Calf," Exodus 20:3-6; 31: 18; 32; 34

Supplies- sensory table and/or individual tubs filled with corn meal

----

*Sensory Center- As you work with the corn meal, say: "God is loving and forgiving. I will worship only Him."

❖ ❖ ❖ ❖ ❖ ❖ ❖ ❖ ❖ ❖ ❖ ❖ ❖

Special Needs Learning Center Set Up
Concept-Listening (week 26)

Preschool/ Primary and Intermediate/ Middle School:

Supplies- trampoline, therapy ball, hula hoop, play tunnel, scooter, spinning disc

----

*Gross Motor Center- Move on the big equipment while practicing this Bible verse: "There shall no evil befall thee, neither any plague comes…" Psalms 91:10

Supplies- animal (snakes, fish, frog, insect) puzzles, games and toys; set out simple puzzles and activities for younger children and more complex puzzles and games for older kids

---

*Fine Motor Center- When King Pharaoh did not listen to God, God sent the plagues. Some of the plagues were a snake, fish that died, frogs and insects everywhere. Find these animals on your puzzles, games and toys.

Supplies-preschool/ primary: " The Lord is my Helper" worksheet, "Listen Up Ears" cut outs, pipe cleaners, crayons, glue, people cut outs; intermediate/ middle school: Pharaoh/ Moses Finger puppets, craft sticks, glue markers

---

*Art Center- preschool/ primary- God helped and protected Moses and the Israelites. Pharaoh and the Egyptians did not listen to God. He sent the plagues of Egypt. We can listen to and follow God. Make listening ears and helper faces.

---

 *Art Center- intermediate/ middle school- God helped and protected Moses and the Israelites. Pharaoh and the Egyptians did not listen to God. He sent the plagues of Egypt. We can listen to and follow God. Make finger puppets of Pharaoh, Moses, the Israelites and Egyptians.

Supplies- Children's Bibles and storybooks set out on mat with cushions. Stuffed snake, frogs and fish can be added.

---

*Cuddly Corner/Cozy Corner Center- Read about "The Plagues of Egypt" in Exodus 7:14-25; Exodus 8

Supplies- sensory table and individual tubs filled with dried kidney beans and containers for scooping

---

*Sensory Center- God helps and protects His people. As you work with the beans, think of times and ways that God has protected you and your family when you have listened to Him.

❖ ❖ ❖ ❖ ❖ ❖ ❖ ❖ ❖ ❖ ❖ ❖

Special Needs Learning Center Set Up
Concept-Resurrected (week 27)

Preschool/ Primary and Intermediate/ Middle School:

Supplies- mini trampolines, play tunnel, spinning disc, therapy balls, scooter

----

*Gross Motor Center- Can you "rise up" on the big equipment? Now, practice this Bible verse: "…and the dead in Christ shall rise first." 1Thessalonians 4:16

Supplies- Easter puzzles and building manipulatives (various blocks and linking toys)

----

*Fine Motor Center- Build the tomb that Jesus was buried in. Mary Magdalene and her friends were so sad that Jesus had died. When they saw that the stone in front of the tomb had been rolled away, they cried "Jesus is gone."

----

*Supplies-**preschool/primary**: butterfly cut-outs, Easter pictures, glue sticks, dot markers, crayons, pastel construction paper sheets; **intermediate/ middle school**: "He is risen" cut-outs, Easter pictures, glue sticks, dot markers, crayons, pastel construction paper sheet;*

----

*Art Center- Make a beautiful Easter card to give to a friend. Fold your paper in half and glue your Easter message inside. Add your Easter cut out to the front of your card. Tell your friend that "Jesus is alive and resurrected from the dead."

Supplies- Easter stories and Children's Bibles set out on story mats

----

*Cuddly Corner/Cozy Corner Center- Read the Bible story of the Resurrection. Matthew 28; Mark 16: 1-18; Luke 24; John 20

Supplies- sensory table and/or individual tubs filled with cotton balls, small Easter baskets

----

*Sensory Center- Jesus was "resurrected" from the dead. This means that Jesus became alive.   He would soon rise into the heavens. Fill your Easter baskets with heavenly clouds. If we believe in Jesus, we will go to heaven someday.

Special Needs Learning Center Set Up
Concept-Praise (week 28)

Preschool/ Primary and Intermediate/ Middle School:

Supplies- mini trampoline, therapy ball, play tunnel, scooter, disc

----

*Gross Motor Center- Pretend to travel to Bethlehem by jumping, crawling, scooting or bouncing on the big equipment. Practice this Bible verse with praise as you travel: "Unto you is born this day…a Savior, Which is Christ the Lord." Luke 2:11.

Supplies- Christmas versions of puzzles, dominoes, bingo and other games, red/green building toys, nativity (farm) animal puzzles

----

*Fine Motor Center- Jesus came to earth to save us. When we celebrate Christmas, we remember His birth. We praise His name. Have fun with the Christmas puzzles and games. Remember and give praise to Jesus as you play.

Supplies-**preschool primary**- *large sheep cut outs, cotton balls, green filler paper, dark blue construction paper, glue, crayons – intermediate/ middle School: small shepherd and sheep cut outs, cotton balls, dark blue construction paper, glue, markers, crayons, Christmas coloring sheets*

----

*Art Center- The shepherds heard about the birth of Jesus from an angel, while they watched their sheep by night. Make the sheep that the shepherds cared for. Jesus came into the world to care for us, as a shepherd cares for his sheep. We can give praise to God for this!

Supplies- Children's Bible and Christmas books set out on a mat with cushions. Stuffed "nativity" animals (cow donkey, sheep) may be added.

----

*Cuddly Corner/Cozy Corner Center- Read the the story of "The Visit of the Shepherds," Luke 2:3

Supplies- sensory table or individual tubs filled with hay or straw, farm animals and nativity figures

----

*Sensory Center- The shepherds traveled to see the Christ child. They fell on their knees to worship Him. They were filled with praise! Set up the nativity scene with animals and figures. Fall on your knees and say a prayer to Jesus.

❖ ❖ ❖ ❖ ❖ ❖ ❖ ❖ ❖ ❖ ❖ ❖ ❖

<u>Special Needs Learning Center Set Up</u>
<u>Concept-Seeking (week 29)</u>

<u>Preschool/ Primary and Intermediate/ Middle School:</u>

Supplies-mini trampolines, therapy balls, spinning disc, scooter, play tunnel, tumbling mat

---

*Gross Motor Center- Practice and try to memorize this Bible verse: "For the Son of Man is come to seek and to save the lost." Luke 19:10

Supplies-wooden blocks, cubes, stained glass builders, legos, Lincoln logs, other building manipulatives

---

*Fine Motor Center- Build Zacchaeus' house. Jesus looked up at Zacchaeus in the tree and said: "Zacchaeus come down. I'm going to your house today." Jesus had come to save Zacchaeus. He had brought him salvation.

Supplies-paper lunch sacks, markers, crayons, stamps and stamp pads, yarn ties, coins

---

*Art Center- It is never too late to invite Jesus into our hearts. We can seek Jesus at any time. Decorate the money bag that Zacchaeus used to collect money from all of the people. When Zacchaeus saw Jesus, he decided to give half of his money to the poor and to pay back those he had cheated. Fill your bag with coins. What will *you* do with your money??

Supplies-children's books and Bibles set out on story mat with cushions and people puppets to reenact the story

---

*Cuddly Corner/Cozy Corner Center-Read the story about "Zacchaeus Wants to See Jesus." Use people puppets to act out the story.

Supplies-sensory table and/ or individual sensory tubs filled with soil, gardening tools, seeds and planting cups

----

*Sensory Center- Zacchaeus wanted to see Jesus. He climbed up into a tree so that he could see above all the people. As you plant your seed, picture it growing into a "little tree." Let your "tree" remind you of how much you want to see Jesus. Be a "Jesus Seeker."

Special Needs Learning Center Set Up
Concept-Caring (week 30)

Preschool/ Primary and Intermediate/ Middle School:

Supplies- mini trampoline, therapy ball, spinning discs, scooter, hula hoop, play tunnel, small balls

----

*Gross Motor Center- Practice this Bible verse with your hand on your heart: "Thou shall love the Lord thy God with all thy heart." Luke 10:27

Supplies- various puzzles with people; simpler puzzles should be used for younger children; more challenging jigsaws should be used for older kids

----

*Fine Motor Center- As you put together these "people puzzles," think about ways that you can be caring to your neighbor. Name some ways that you can "love your neighbor as yourself."

Supplies- colorful construction paper folded in halves, cut out hearts, heart stickers, Band-Aids, markers/crayons, glue
----
*Art Center- We should be loving and caring to everyone who needs our help, no matter what church they go to or what color their skin is. Make a Good Samaritan card with caring hearts and bandages. Give your card to someone who is hurting or needs help.

Supplies- Children's Bibles and storybooks set out on mat with cushions
----
*Cuddly Corner/Cozy Corner Center- Read the story of "The Good Samaritan," Luke 10:25-37

Supplies- sensory table or individual tubs filled with shaving cream, cups, containers, utensils
----
*Sensory Center- Write these letters in the shaving cream using your fingers or a utensil: "S-a-m-a-r-i-t-a-n." How can you be a Good Samaritan?

❖ ❖ ❖ ❖ ❖ ❖ ❖ ❖ ❖ ❖ ❖ ❖ ❖

Special Needs Learning Center Set Up
Concept- Kindness (week 31)

Preschool/ Primary and Intermediate/ Middle School:

Supplies-mini trampolines play tunnels, therapy balls, scooter, spinning disc
----
*Gross Motor Center- Say this Bible verse as you move on the big equipment: "The Lord was with Joseph." Genesis 39:21 Remember that God is with you also.

Supplies- various puzzles (wooden framed, foam, jigsaw, linking) with people shapes

----

*Fine Motor Center- Put together the puzzles of people. Think about all of the people you know. Do you treat them with kindness? God tells us that kindness is always the right choice.

Supplies-preschool- cut out white "coats," colorful mixed glitter or tempera paints, brushes; intermediate/middle school- cut out people figures; wiggle eyes, yarn hair, fabric coats, glue, and markers

----

*Art Center- preschool: Paint Joseph's coat. Use as many colors as you can. Joseph's brothers wished that they had a colorful coat, too. They were angry at him. Think about a time that you have felt angry. Did you ask God to help you with your anger?

---

*Art Center- intermediate/ middle school**-** Make Joseph with his new coat. Joseph's brothers wished that they had a colorful coat, too. They were angry at him. Think about a time that you have felt angry. Did you ask God to help you with your anger?

Supplies-Children's Bibles and books set on story mat with cushions

----

*Cuddly Corner/Cozy Corner Center- Read about "The Story of Joseph," Genesis 37

Supplies-sensory table and or individual tubs filled with colorful rocks used for fish tanks, small containers and cup

----

*Sensory Center- Notice the many colors of the rocks. Joseph wore a coat of colors.   He was kind to his brothers even when they were not kind to him.   As you work with the colors, name ways that you can be kind to others.

➡ Checkpoints along the Way

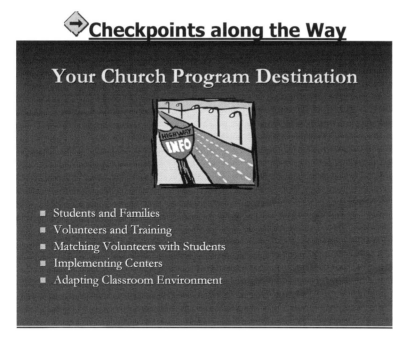

Your Church Program Destination

- Students and Families
- Volunteers and Training
- Matching Volunteers with Students
- Implementing Centers
- Adapting Classroom Environment

Let's review the distance we've covered so far... You now know who some of your students and families might be. You have volunteers in mind and a plan for training them. You have some understanding of how to match volunteers with students with disabilities. You are ready to implement at least one center and gradually add more. You have heard about how to adapt your classroom. God bless you for your desire to be an inclusive church and to open your hearts to the special needs ministry mission. You will be enabling families to kneel before God, so that we can stand before anything.

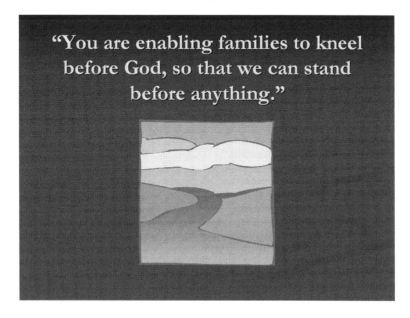

"You are enabling families to kneel before God, so that we can stand before anything."

Some Important Checkpoints

Even churches with the best of intentions can forget to include some of the most important elements in their journey. Consider the following and be sure that they are not overlooked in your mission.

Keep God's Doors Open:

Think of your church as "God's House" and picture Him welcoming in His children. He would welcome in all children regardless of the severity of physical, mental, emotional or behavioral dysfunction. God loves His children as they are. When met with a challenging child, seek to adapt the environment and the teaching methods used to meet the needs of the child's challenges. This requires a careful balance of compassion for the special needs child and family, as well as, expert teaching knowledge. Dismissing a child, from the special needs ministry for any reason, defeats the point of having a special needs ministry at all. God would never turn away a child that knocks on His door. His door is always open.

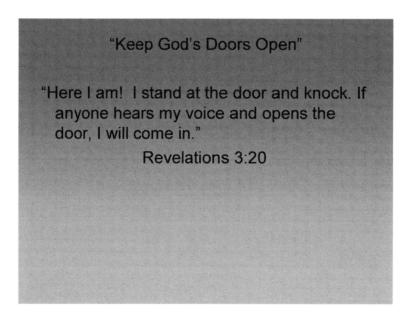

"Keep God's Doors Open"

"Here I am! I stand at the door and knock. If anyone hears my voice and opens the door, I will come in."
Revelations 3:20

Confidentiality:

All negative instances or episodes involving any child in the special needs Sunday school classroom or ministry should be kept confidential. These difficulties should be discussed only with the child's parents and volunteers or staff working specifically with that particular child. Sharing negative facts about a child can be detrimental to both the child and her family.

→ Meeting the Challenge of Behavior in Students with Special Needs

Are you a church that is truly going to open arms to the special needs ministry? Are you going to open arms to all children, including those with disruptive behaviors? In meeting the challenge of behavior in special needs kids, I believe it's important to first develop an understanding of the child's disability. I think one of the questions that I get asked most often, is what happened to your son? Why is he the way that he is? We need to know some **causes of behavioral dysfunction in order to better understand the person.** Some of the causes are:

1. Genetics – There are thousands of complex conditions that doctors are continually studying about today, many have not yet been discovered.

2. A Difficult Birth- Problems during the pregnancy can lead to later troubles in behavior, even in pregnancies where all the doctors' orders are followed and all of the appropriate precautions are taken.

3. Childhood Illness- Encephalitis, meningitis, Reye Syndrome are just a few that can cause brain damage.

4. Traumatic Brain Injury- TBI is one of the leading causes of delays in children.

5. Injury to the Central Nervous System- When the brain and spine are hurt, kids are often left with multiple handicaps.

6. Abnormalities in the Brain- These can usually be detected with types of brain scans, such as MRI's, CAT scans and EEG's.

7. Inherited Predispositions- Tendencies that are passed on from one generation to the next might contribute, as well.

8. Early Traumatic Experience- Abuse is usually the cause, here. My husband is a prosecuting attorney and tells me that "shaken baby syndrome" has become more and more prevalent.

9. Chemical Imbalance- This condition can lead to anxiety, depression and emotional problems.

10. Environmental Problems- Not all of us live in environmentally clean and safe atmospheres. Toxic sites can lead to injuries of the brain.

11. Unknown- I've added the "unknown" category, because often times children are "undiagnosed." Parents and Doctors really don't know the cause of the disability.

It is crucial also to **avoid common misconceptions about inappropriate behaviors in children**. Here are some of our misconceptions:

1. ***The behavior is purposeful/ intentional-*** We might think to ourselves, this child has a bad attitude and is willfully choosing to act out. Kids with disabilities do have conditions that affect their behavior. For example, a child with epilepsy might become confused and hyperactive following a seizure that isn't even visible to us. A child with TBI or traumatic brain injury might have aggressive outbursts.
2. ***The child has the ability to control or change his behavior on command-*** We ask a child to do something and she doesn't adhere. I asked my very bright, daughter, when she was eight years old, to please stop absent- mindedly kicking her foot against the chair in front of her. "I can't control myself," she said to me. "You ARE the person who controls yourself," I said back. "No Mom, my DNA controls me," was her response. Of course, I quickly reminded her that the teacher who taught her about genetics also covered environmental factors, which meant that she could learn. This is not always the case for kids with neurological or social deficits. *Yes, they are capable of learning and changing, but not always on command.* For instance, a child with autism might vocalize loudly at inappropriate times. His neurological condition is influencing his behavior. Something internally is going on with him.
3. ***The parent is at Fault-*** Sometimes we blame parents. We think there needs to be more discipline, more consistency in the home. Although these factors can help, they are not the cause of the behavior.
4. ***Medication is the answer-*** (How we as parents, sometimes wish that it was...like at 3am!!) Often times, medication does work well and it is certainly needed for many conditions. However, it is not "magic". Sometimes kids develop a tolerance to it, and it stops working. Sometimes it causes side effects that are worse than the actual behavior itself.

There are many **classifications for kids with special needs.** These are all conditions that can affect behavior. These classifications are taken from the state and federal guidelines under the Individualized Disabilities Educational Act (IDEA). In order for students with disabilities to receive services in special education and to have individualized educational plans, the school district is required to evaluate the student and determine a classification.

1. Learning Disabled

2. Mentally Retarded

3. Speech Impaired

4. Language Impaired

5. Emotionally Disturbed

6. Autism

7. Health Impaired

8. Physically Challenged

9. Hearing Impaired

10. Visually Impaired

11. Deaf Blind

12. Multi-Disabled

13. Developmentally Delayed

14. Traumatic Brain Injury

15. Gifted

(That last one is a surprise.) A lot of people don't realize that "gifted" kids are kids with special needs, too. They don't necessarily have IEP's in the school districts but are often receiving special services in the form of an accelerated program.

We now need to identify the needs of the child. Looking at all of these different categories that I have just mentioned and keeping in mind the causes of and misconceptions about behavior, we're going to focus on what it is that the child with disabilities really needs when he is misbehaving. I always say to myself when I see kids who are acting out, "What is it that the child is seeking? What's going on internally with this child that's causing him to behave in this way?" There's a saying that goes: "Give a child what she needs, not what she wants."

Kids with deficits often need what it is that they are lacking. A non verbal child needs to be provided with ways to communicate. A non ambulatory child needs to be provided with mobility options. A non social child needs to be provided with opportunities to socialize.

Consider the following examples of behavioral dysfunctions. Can you figure out what the child in each situation is seeking and how you would meet his needs?

The situations are:

A child with autism bites teacher and classmates.

A child with developmental delays and hearing impairment talks out in class.

A child with ADHD cannot sit still; runs and paces around the room.

A child with language impairments hits and pulls hair.

A child with complex disabilities cries out loudly for long periods of time.

How would you deal with these real life scenarios? While, there is no single answer, the suggestions on the following pages have been found to be beneficial in individual cases. (Record some of your initial thoughts here.)

_____
_____
_____
_____
_____
_____
_____
_____
_____
_____
_____
_____
_____
_____
_____
_____
_____
_____
_____
_____
_____
_____

BEHAVIORAL SCENARIOS

What do you think that the child in each situation might be seeking? How would you meet his or her needs?

A child with autism tries to bite the teacher

_____
_____
_____
_____
_____
_____
_____

A child with developmental delays and hearing impairment talks out in class

_____
_____
_____
_____
_____
_____

A child with ADHD cannot sit still; runs and paces around the room

_____
_____
_____
_____
_____
_____

A child with language impairments tries to hit and pull hair

_____
_____
_____
_____
_____
_____

A child with complex disabilities cries out loudly for long periods of time

_____
_____
_____
_____
_____
_____

The child with autism who bites teacher and classmates:

*might be over stimulated and need some down time in a quiet area of the classroom with a volunteer.

*might be frustrated and need a chance to release frustration perhaps with some play dough or clay or through the expression of an art activity.

*might be anxious and need a routine to be in place as well as ample time to make changes.

*may be seeking a sensory need that isn't being met, and can become engaged in a sensory table or tub filled with a tactile substance such as sand or water.

*could have a condition called oral perseverance or a fixation with putting things in the mouth and should be given something appropriate to bite onto. It could be a snack that the child likes and responds to. It could be a piece of chewing gum. For a younger child, it might be a "teether" or chewing toy.

*It's important not to over-react to a situation like this and to notify parents in a sensitive and tactful way.

The child with developmental delays and hearing impairment who talks out in class:

A Child with Developmental Delays and Hearing Impairment Talks out in Class

*needs a chance to express himself, perhaps through a language center, an art center or a music center.
*may not have heard or understood the direction and needs a visual to hold his attention. He should also be placed at the front of the classroom.
*might respond to a "special signal" such as hand clapping or pointing to the ears or a simple touch on the shoulder.
*can be redirected while talking (ex. "Thank you for telling us about your dog. I know that Jesus loves him, too. Jesus would like us now to say a prayer.)
*responds to affirmations (ex. "That's excellent listening that you've been doing. Now is a good time for you to tell your story.)

*Talk to parents about their wishes for their hearing impaired child. Some are in favor of sign language. Others are not. It's a personal choice.

The child with ADHD who cannot sit still; runs and paces around the room:

*is seeking activity and needs to be given opportunities to be active. Gross motor activities could include a mini trampoline in the classroom to be used for a break time, a crawling tunnel, scooter, or big ball. Teachers can provide appropriate times for the whole class to be active and move about. It may be that occasionally, we need to let this child walk about with a helper for a short period of time.
* benefits from clay and tactile toys to be used to maintain the child's attention at the table.
*can be given a special chair such as a beanbag or bubble chair to help him remain seated.
*can use a "transition toy" to be a motivator as he moves from one activity to the next.

*Respite for these parents is really necessary. Church volunteers can support them in this way.

The child with language impairments hits and pulls hair:

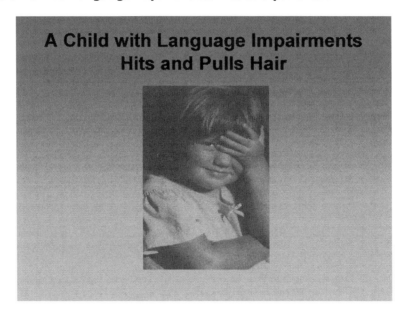

*is likely frustrated because she cannot talk the way that she would like to. We need to surround her with alternative ways of communicating. Sign language, language or picture cards, photographs, PECS or writing with symbols made by Mayer and Johnson is a computerized program that helps children to communicate. Ablenet makes many communication devices. Many times families have these devices at home.

*needs other modes of expressing herself through art, music, or a game.

*might need some "down time" in the book corner or cozy area of the classroom.

*might need to be with two volunteers if the behaviors are dangerous.

*can be kept at "arms length distance" from peers and volunteers during problematic behaviors.

*needs parents to be involved in equipping teachers with information about their child.

*Be especially kind to these parents. They are probably feeling very badly about their child's behavior.

The child with complex disabilities, who cries loudly for long periods of time:

*is seeking comfort and soothing. She needs a calming area and activity, such as the story center, with cushions, books and a blanket.
*needs diversion with a favorite toy or game.
* might enjoy soft music or a quiet video.
* may, depending on her cognitive level, respond to a "feelings chart" with photographs of children to identify her mood.

*All of these ideas are super ways to help children get what it is that they are seeking. When we look to meet their needs, we are looking to fill in or complete that which they are lacking.

*Next, in controlling challenging behaviors, there are some classroom management strategies that I have found to be very helpful for children with disabilities. Four components, specifically, work well with student behavior, and organization.

First is the **classroom arrangement or the adaptation of the classroom environment (** page 46**).**

It is one example of how you can arrange your classroom. The point that I want to emphasize on behavior is that you want for your classroom to be clutter free. Extra stimuli can create problems for kids with attention issues. You also want to arrange your classroom in a similar fashion each week for children who need routine. You want for your center activities to be clearly labeled with instructions for children and adults so that adults can keep children on task. If the adults don't know what the task at hand is, they can't keep the kids focused. If you have some one very meticulous in your church, they would be a good person to have set up these centers. I was the person that had been overseeing this at our church for years. I'm pretty sure that I drove some people a little crazy with wanting the classrooms to be just right for the kids, but I had seen how well they did in an organized atmosphere, so I had no regrets about doing so.

Second, I encourage the **utilization of practical teaching tools to maintain the child's attention**. These are all of the "attention getters", visuals, props, and devices that can be used both to get the point across and to engage the kid's interests. When kids are engaged, it is because their needs are being met. When their needs are being met, their behavioral deficits are less visible. *Some examples of teaching tools are: storyboards with felt pieces* (These are made by Betty Lukens.*), posters, pictures, photographs* (Curriculum for this is listed on page 31.) You can also make your own large printed posters with poems and songs for kids to read, *real objects* that kids can hold as a story is being told, *costumes/hats* that can be placed on/around a child (depending on the sensory toleration of the child), *communication devices*, such as buttons or recorders that allow a non- verbal or child with limited speech to make a statement (These are made by Ablenet.), *picture cards* used by the student to indicate a need or want (PECS or "writing with symbols" have good programs for this. They are made by Mayer and Johnson.) You can use *photograph cards* to make a schedule for children to follow along, *signing and gesturing*, for example, "Everyone sign: Jesus Loves Me," and signals such as "1,2 ,3, eyes on me, 1, 2, eyes on you" can help kids to attend.

Third, **learn from parents**. They truly are the experts on their children. The following are confidential forms that can be distributed to parents. They are to be used by classroom teachers to benefit the child in the classroom.

The *parent questionnaire* gives parents the chance to write helpful information about their child's needs. The information goes into an individual file for each student. Parents can also add information, such as school goals or doctors letters. The volunteer that is working specifically with that particular child reviews these details (page 163).

The *special instructions form* is for parents to write Sunday instructions for volunteers. It's a place for parents to jot down food restrictions, any changes in behavior or mood, toileting needs for the hour, etc. (page 167).

The *medication release form* is a legal document and waiver used occasionally for kids who need to take medication during class (page 165).

The *special needs ministry evaluation form* is a survey to be used at the end of the year to improve upon the program. It's important to get feedback from both parents and volunteers and to make changes based on the comments (page 169).

The final and most important component to managing behavior in the special needs Sunday classroom is to maintain **a Christ like atmosphere.**

Model appropriate behaviors. Be positive and firm with children. "I love the way that you are going to do this art project, right now." "You can choose to use blue or green. You choose. Which one?" "First sit down, and then have the markers."

Be respectful of all children and find a way for all children to have a successful learning experience. I can't say it any better than a student with special needs said while giving a testimonial during Sunday school. In the words of Alex: "No matter if you are a snowboarder, or skier, or a swimmer, or a basketball player...you can still praise God."

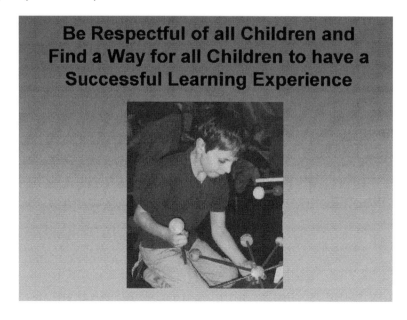

Be flexible and allow for differences. A parent of a student with disabilities calmly explained to me that her child had "oral perseveration" or a fixation with putting things in her mouth. Because she has no oral weakness or problems with chewing or choking, she's encouraged to keep a small pine needle in her mouth. This is different, but it meets this child's sensory needs. It allows her to stay calm and focused in the classroom. At Christmas time, this child, along with the rest of the class, gathered to make holiday wreaths out of tree greens. At the end of the project, one of the volunteers turned to me and said, "Well, she came in with pine and went out with cedar." I thought to myself, now that's true flexibility.

Provide a Sense of Caring Throughout. My own son, Zach, who is now very cognitively impaired, often comes to class fatigued from seizures. He usually heads straight for the cozy corner or the relaxing area in class. One Sunday, though, he noticed a place that looked even more comfortable. From across the room, he spotted a beautiful black fringed shawl that was worn by a volunteer. He sat himself down on her lap, wrapped the shawl around the two of them and went to sleep. In his mind, I'm certain that he was thinking, "Isn't great that this teacher had my family room blanket here ready and waiting for me?" "My church knows just what I need, open arms wrapped around me." My prayer for you today is that you too will open your arms to the special needs ministry."

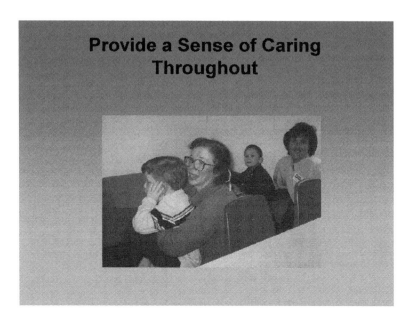

Provide a Sense of Caring Throughout

We can be compassionate when we develop a connection with these families.

➡**How to Stay Connected with the Special Needs Family:**

#1. <u>Get to know the family</u>. Call them. Meet with them. Email them. Find out the best way to communicate with them and what works for their schedule.

#2. <u>Become familiar with their Needs.</u> If you know the child's diagnosis or disability, read about it. Otherwise, let families share with you at their pace and their own discretion.   We all come to terms with our children's disability in different ways. Let families tell you their child's diagnosis. Ask how you can be supportive of their child's needs.

A side note on asking about disabilities: learning to question appropriately, using language that is worded tactfully and considered to be "politically correct" can be a daunting task. When doing so keep this story in mind:

Years ago when teaching a school classroom of first and second graders, I felt obliged to advise them on "questioning skills." We had been studying careers and would soon have members of the community coming into our classroom to share with us about their occupations. As we practiced our skills, I encouraged questions such as "How do you feel about your job?" "What equipment do you use in your job?" "How much schooling did your job require?" "Would you choose this job over if you had the opportunity?"

One student in particular, who was gifted, was intrigued by the question of "How much money do you make?" I immediately did some quick thinking and talked to the students about being sure that the question they asked would be one that would make the person "feel comfortable." I used the examples of "How old are you ?," or "How much do you weigh ?,"as being questions that might NOT make a person "feel comfortable." "Before asking a question," I stressed, "Ask yourself, is this a question that will make the person feel comfortable?"

The next day, our first career spokesperson entered the classroom. The questioning began well. Then Michael's hand went up…With complete confidence he asked when called upon, "Would you feel comfortable telling us how much money you make?" If you are like Michael and simply must ask, do as he did and ask with some sensitivity and a sense of genuine interest!!

#3. Develop an understanding and an appreciation for some of the daily struggles:
*There's a feeling of grief and continual loss for what "might have been."
*Social situations are difficult; it sometimes seems as if there are few places that children with disabilities can participate.
*Having to be a constant advocate is tiring; to explain over and over again and to defend over and over again our children.
*Issues of friendship or perhaps having a child who has not a single friend is a reality.
*Being a good parent to siblings can be challenging. Often, the focus is on the special needs child.
*Maintaining a strong marriage under stressful circumstances is hard to do. The divorce rate is high for families with special needs.

#4. Pray specifically for their needs. Ask for their prayer requests.

#5. Be there in times of crisis-
*Medical emergencies/ procedures are frequent for many families.
*Loss of health care benefits or caretaking services can be devastating.
*Problems at school/ school system are common. We were once told that school wasn't the place for our child.
*New diagnosis and coming to terms with the hard facts can be a struggle and can take a long time.
*There is the ongoing worry of "How will I continue to care for my child?" This thought often hits parents when their child is in his teenage years.

#6. Find ways for families to become an integral part of the church
*Provide partners in prayer who can get together with and minister to parents.
*Set up a prayer support group for special needs families; some groups meet monthly. A men's and women's group works well.
*Provide some childcare so that parents can attend adult church functions.
*MOST IMPORTANTLY, provide volunteers so that children can participate in Sunday school and parents can attend church.

7. Provide Community Outreach for the Special Needs Ministry

Throughout this book, I have maintained the idea that families with disabilities will come to your church if they know that there is a place for them. I believe this, because I belong to one of those families…who church would not be a possibility for otherwise. I have also had the joy of seeing many families enter the church as a result of this ministry.

What about the families, though, who don't come? Even with the invitation of a special needs ministry, could the church still be missing some folks? Is it too much of a struggle for the single Mom to get her child with disabilities to church in the morning? Consider the lengthy process that it takes for some families with special needs to simply leave the house... including medications, home medical procedures, feeding routines, assistance with personal care and behavioral management of neurological, cognitive and emotional conditions. Is it going to be too much of an effort for some? How about those who wonder why God would allow disability to occur in the first place and consequently have no interest in church? The stressful dynamics of having a child with disabilities can make families appear to be more dysfunctional.

Can the church provide outreach to this community? Can they reach those who are unable to see Jesus in their lives? Can congregants connect with families with disabilities who are overwhelmed with their situations and do not have the energy, motivation or interest in the institution of the church? For these families, it may be necessary to enter their world and to meet them on their own terms.

Reggie McNeal, author of The Present Future says that "Jesus' strategy was to go where people were already…" Can your church be Jesus in the world of:

1. **Homes** - provide support by having several volunteers visit families in their homes, if they are unable to make it to Sunday services.
2. **Schools and Residential Facilities** - ask if there are service projects that a group of church volunteers can participate in to help people with disabilities.
3. **Public Places** - hold support groups off campus to attract outsiders.
4. **Partnerships** - join together with disability organizations and other churches with similar missions.
5. **Mentorships** - go beyond the church walls to assist a family by attending IEP, health services, or guardianship meetings.

After all, the church is not a building but a people. Encourage people to give the good news of Jesus through serving others.

Special Needs Sunday School Teaching Schedule
Month of_____

Date	Lead Teacher	Medical Professional	Therapist	Support Staff	Peer Tutors
____	_____	_____	_____	_____	_____
				_____	_____
				_____	_____

Date	Lead Teacher	Medical Professional	Therapist	Support Staff	Peer Tutors
____	_____	_____	_____	_____	_____
				_____	_____
				_____	_____

Date	Lead Teacher	Medical Professional	Therapist	Support Staff	Peer Tutors
____	_____	_____	_____	_____	_____
				_____	_____
				_____	_____

Date	Lead Teacher	Medical Professional	Therapist	Support Staff	Peer Tutors
____	_____	_____	_____	_____	_____
				_____	_____
				_____	_____

Date	Lead Teacher	Medical Professional	Therapist	Support Staff	Peer Tutors
____	_____	_____	_____	_____	_____
				_____	_____
				_____	_____

Special Needs Sunday School Teaching Schedule

Month_____   _____   Lead Teacher

Date_____   _____   Medical Professional

_____   Therapist

_____   Support Staff

_____   Support Staff

Month_____   _____   Lead Teacher

Date_____   _____   Medical Professional

_____   Therapist

_____   Support Staff

_____   Support Staff

Month_____   _____   Lead Teacher

Date_____   _____   Medical Professional

_____   Therapist

_____   Support Staff

_____   Support Staff

Month_____   _____   Lead Teacher

Date_____   _____   Medical Professional

_____   Therapist

_____   Support Staff

_____   Support Staff

Month_____   _____   Lead Teacher

Date_____   _____   Medical Professional

_____   Therapist

_____   Support Staff

_____   Support Staff

Parent Questionnaire
CONFIDENTIAL

Parent's Name_____

Child's Name_____

Child's Birth Date_____

❖ Describe your child's special needs (Explain any treatments, therapies or adaptations that your child responds well to, e.g. sensory integration therapy, PECS/picture exchange communication system, sign language, etc._____

_____

_____

_____

❖ When working with your child, are there any life threatening, emergencies, or safety issues that classroom volunteers should be aware of?_____

_____

_____

_____

❖ What are your child's strengths and weaknesses?_____

_____

_____

_____

_____

❖ What goals (short and long term) would you like to set for your child that can be achieved in the special needs Sunday school ministry?_____

_____

_____

_____

_____

❖ What level of curriculum do you think is appropriate for your child (2-3 years, 4-5 years, 1st grade, 2nd grade, etc)?_____

_____

❖ Is it your goal to include your child into all or part of the regular Sunday school classroom?_____

_____

_____

❖ List any special instructions (include toileting/changing, medical diets/food restrictions, medication, etc.)_____

_____

Special Needs Ministry
Authorization for Administration of Medication at Class and Release

Student's Name_____Birthdate_____

_____

Name of Medication	Dosage	Method of Administration	Time of day to be Given
_____	_____	_____	_____
_____	_____	_____	_____
_____	_____	_____	_____

Possible Side Effects of Medication: _____

1. I request and authorize that the above named student be administered the above identified medication during the Special Needs Class in accordance with the instructions indicated. The instructions will remain in effect until changed by me in writing, delivered to one of the Lead Teachers of the Special Needs Class. There exists a valid health reason which makes administration of the medication advisable during the Special Needs Class.

2. I agree that any of the personnel of the Special Needs Class who without compensation or the expectation of compensation administers the above identified medication in accordance with the instructions indicated, renders emergency care to the above named student during the Special Needs Class, or who participates in transporting not for compensation the above named student to a location where emergency medical care can be provided shall not be liable for civil damages resulting from any act or omission in the administering of the medication, in the rendering of such emergency care or in the transporting of such student other than acts or omissions constituting gross negligence or willful or wanton misconduct (RDW 4.24.300)

3. I certify that I am the parent, legal guardian or other person in legal control of the above named student.

MEDICATIONS MUST BE SUPPLIED TO THE SPECIAL NEEDS CLASS IN A CONTAINER CLEARLY LABELED WITH THE NAME OF THE MEDICATION.

_____   _____
Parent/Legal Guardian's Signature   Date of Signature

(   ) _____
Phone number at which I may be reached during the Special Needs Class.

SUNDAY SCHOOL SPECIAL NEEDS MINISTRY
DATE_____

NAME	SPECIAL INSTRUCTIONS

Special Needs Ministry Evaluation

Name_____

1. What have you liked about this year's special needs ministry?

   _____

   _____

   _____

2. What are your suggestions for improvement?

   _____

   _____

   _____

3. Will you participate in the special needs ministry again next year?

   _____

   If yes, how often will you volunteer?

   _____

   _____

   If you have a child or children (student or students with special needs or typical peers) that will participate in the ministry, please list name(s) and age(s).

   _____

   _____

4. Do you have additional comments?

   _____

   _____

   _____

5. May we print your comments in a parent handbook for new families?

   _____

   _____

   _____

Your Arrival

Having a child with special needs presents ongoing challenges and daily struggles for many families. It can, at times, be a heartbreaking experience. If we ask Him to, God will see us through the most difficult times. He will show us what a blessing and gift our special children are. Our children teach us about compassion and unconditional love ----- two very Christ like qualities. May we learn from them and rely on our faith in Christ to remain strong in God's kingdom.

This Sunday hour is a gift from God to special families that is only possible with the help of churches, who have both knowledge about and compassion for children with disabilities. **Churches that enable learners with disabilities enable God to work in the lives of families with special needs. "I have made you wonderfully," God says to all of His children in Psalm 119.** Let us go forward and teach His wonderful children.

> "And the Lord, He it is that does go before thee; he will be with thee, he will not fail thee, neither forsake thee: fear not, neither be dismayed. Deuteronomy 31:8
>
> May God guide you along the way,
> Amy Rapada
> rapada@email.com

About the Author

My Experiences with Special Needs Children

As an elementary school teacher, curriculum specialist, coordinator of special needs ministries, and as a parent, I have been very closely involved in the lives of children with special needs for 20 years. I was fortunate to enter the teaching field at a time when Outcome Based Education Programs were being piloted. Consequently, under the Inclusion Model, I taught to and wrote/ developed curriculum specifically for children of special populations. I had many students with significant, moderate and mild disabilities in my classrooms. I reinforced their individualized educational plans, provided behavioral interventions, and collaborated with specialists in order to accommodate their needs. I designed corrective curriculum that was targeted toward those with deficits in order to increase standardized and alternative testing results and implemented enrichment programs for accelerated learners. I have always had a real heart for children with differences and my highest goal and accomplishment as an educator was and is to enable all children to have a successful learning experience.

As a regular classroom teacher and Sunday school teacher it was my honor to teach to a diverse group of children. I sought to meet the individual needs of each of the children that I came into contact with. It was a joy for me to interact with, model to and develop a positive rapport with these kids. I enjoyed creating, adapting, and implementing curriculum for them. I have always appreciated the uniqueness of every child with special needs and aimed to help all children reach their greatest potential.

While my formal teaching experiences have been very valuable, I believe that my experiences outside the classroom are what best equip me for sharing the good news of the special needs ministry. It is only as a parent that I have learned the lessons of round the clock caretaking, unwavering determination, and unconditional love. God has blessed me with the wonderful and challenging experiences of having two children with special needs. My son, Zach's pervasive and progressive disabilities have allowed me to master in depth how to creatively teach under extreme circumstances. My daughter Emily's gifted abilities have taken me to detailed understandings of the learning process. I value every teaching opportunity and believe there is no child too difficult to teach.

172

My Qualifications for Presenting at your Church or Conference

Knowledge and compassion are the two strongest qualifications that I have for training and presenting special education workshops. My educational background and professional and life experiences have helped me to acquire a great deal of knowledge about children with disabilities. I have studied physical, mental, social, behavioral, language, sensory, learning and health impairments, as well as causes and treatments of dysfunction, effective teaching strategies and therapeutic measures. I am very familiar with children's Christian curriculum and skilled at adapting it to fit the needs of special learners. I carry with me knowledge of classroom management, structure and organization, and practical teaching tools used to control challenging behaviors.

I know well how to recruit, train, and prepare volunteers, and how to oversee and execute special programs and events. I have strong administrative skills and have created from scratch, along with the support of many others, a number of church special needs ministries. Because, I know the job of a special needs leader in the church and have continually sought to change and improve upon it, I am able to share valuable insights with others.

I have a passion and love for children and am genuinely interested in and want to understand every student. I care deeply for their families and strive to be perceptive and aware of their personal situations and values. I relate well with and can appreciate their struggles. I feel a special connection with these families and try to use that information to create awareness in others. I am able to work as a team with volunteers and staff and want to encourage a positive and caring environment. It is a pleasure for me to motivate and inspire the gifts and talents that volunteers bring with them into the special needs ministry. I always pray that I will lead in a Christ like way.

Please contact me at:

Amy Rapada, MA Ed.
Special Needs Ministries
rapada@email.com

➡️About Special Needs Ministries...................

"........A fantastic addition to Children's Ministries. The program reaches out to families both within and outside the church community. Parents are able to worship with other adults for perhaps the first time!"
    Jenny Whalen, Preschool Teacher

"This is a team of skilled participants from a variety of backgrounds, and it's been a nice way for me to share some of my work with my church family."
    Janine Smith, Occupational Therapist

"This ministry is a huge blessing to all involved."
    Sue Craik, Director of Children's Ministries

".....The special needs ministry has given so many kids a great place to learn about God...."
    Karen Evenson, Pediatric Physical Therapist

"I love to see the children participate.....hear them sing.....read the Bible story....and just watch the expressions on their faces when they talk about Jesus. They make me feel special."
    Marie Harley, Special Education Teacher

"I think the program was very successful and hope it is an inspiration to all and continues to grow."
    Randy Fullerton, Paramedic

"I like the structure (of the ministry), the way the Bible is being taught to my special children, the music, crafts, EVERYTHING!!"
    Sigrid Barnickel, Family Medicine Physician & Parent of Special Needs Children

"It was great to see the children excited about the various activities and parents enthusiastic about the program."
    Cathy McGinn, Elementary School Teacher

"I think every member of our church family should have the opportunity to receive the blessing that comes from working with these terrific kids."
    Robin Bennett, Preschool Teacher

"The children were so much fun ......each so unique."
    Jeff Vavra, Nurse Anesthesiologist

"I am thrilled that mom's and dad's of special needs kids have an opportunity to worship our dear Lord, knowing that their child is being cared for by knowledgeable, God loving people."
    Sue McKain, School Occupational Therapist

➡Other Resources

* ***The Spiritual Resource Ministry Program Guide***
  by the San Francisco Church of Christ

* ***Developmentally Appropriate Practices for Children***
  by the National Educational Association

* ***What to Do About Your Brain Injured Child or Your Brain-Damaged, Mentally Retarded, Mentally Deficient, Cerebral-Palsied, Spastic, Flaccid, Rigid, Epileptic, Autistic, Athetoid, Hyperactive, Down's Child***
  by Glenn Doman

* ***The American Sign Language Dictionary***
  by Martin L.A. Sternberg

* ***EP Exceptional Parent Magazine***
  www.eparent.com

* ***Exceptional Teaching***
  by Jim Pierson

* ***Special Needs, Special Ministry***
  by Louise Tucker Jones, Jim Pierson, Pat Verbal and Joni Eareckson Tada

* ***Playing the Hand that's Dealt to you —A Guide for Parents of Children with Special Needs***
  by Janet Morel

* ***Special Parent, Special Child***
  by Tom Sullivan

****Ten Things That Every Child with Autism Wishes you Knew***
  by Ellen Notbohm

* ***Through The Roof- a Guide to Assist Churches in Developing an Effective Disability Outreach***
  by Joni Eeareckson Tada, Steve Miller and Joni and Friends

****All God's Children-***
  by Gene Newman and Joni Eareckson Tada

****Let All the Children Come to Me***
  by MaLesa Breeding, Dana Hood, and Jerry Whitworth

****Same Lake, Different Boat***
  by Stephanie O. Hubach

Disability Organizations that Partner with the Church:

*Athletes for Kid's www.athletesforkids.org

*BRIDGE Ministries www.bridgemin.org

* Children's Institute for Learning Differences
www.childrensinstitute.com

*Life Enrichment Options www.leoorganization.org

*Joni and Friends www.joniandfriends.org

*The ARC of King County www.arcofkingco.org

* The Kindering Center www.kindering.org

* The Family Foundation Down's Project www.fundefam.org

*The Salvation Army www.salvationarmyusa.org

*The Wyatt Holliday Foundation www.WyattsHouse.org

*The Young Life Open Door Program http://OpenDoor.younglife.org

Amy Rapada is a curriculum and instruction specialist and special needs church ministry consultant. Amy received her undergraduate degree in education and teaching certification through Seattle Pacific University. She obtained her Masters degree in Education at the University of Washington. She has helped develop special needs programs for many religious communities. A parent of a special needs child, Amy has used her experience and knowledge to publish <u>The Special Needs Ministry Handbook</u>. She was the keynote speaker at the Children with Disabilities Conference, and has presented workshops at the Northwest Christian Education Conference. She served as an elementary school teacher and as a Language Arts Curriculum Specialist in regular, gifted and special education programs for the Highline School District. Over the past seven years, she developed a special needs ministry at Sammamish Presbyterian Church as their special needs ministry coordinator and at Pine Lake Covenant Church in Sammamish, Washington. Currently, Amy consults with and presents to churches and foundations nationally. She is the mother of a 15 year old son, 11 year old daughter and married to a family law attorney.

Needed Worldwide...The Special Needs Ministry is a Mission that Your Church Can Begin Today!

"The Special Needs Ministry Handbook is a "must have" for every congregation that seeks to be obedient to Matthew 19:14. God longs for His people to welcome and embrace **all** children into His church. This book provides clear, thoughtful and practical strategies and tools for developing a successful special needs ministry."

- Children's Ministries Pastor Sandy Klein, M.Ed.
Pine Lake Covenant Church

"This handbook, based on real-life special needs ministry programs in several churches, provides a wealth of practical guidance to churches that are starting or seeking to enhance a special needs ministry for children with disabilities. Through her first-hand experience as a parent of a special needs child, a special education professional and church leader, Amy answers many of the questions churches are asking -- or should be asking – about how the church can lovingly embrace its children with special needs and their families."

- Rev. Donna Whitmore
Chaplain, Bridge Ministries

The Special Needs Ministry Handbook ...
This author gently empowers the reader to move beyond good intentions to appropriate action. Her hands-on approach is time and experience tested. This handbook is the perfect answer to the too often heard lament of "We'd like to reach out to these children, but we don't know where to begin". As we search for effective ways to support children and families, the isolation of the special needs child is often the last to be recognized. Amy Rapada offers the technical and spiritual tips that can generate the best of what a loving community can provide... compassion, inclusion, and acknowledgment of the tender spirit in every human being.

Founder and Executive Director Trina Westerlund
Children's Institute for Learning Differences

Made in the USA
San Bernardino, CA
05 October 2015